What people are saying about *The True Measure of a Man*—

"Should you read this book? If you can relate to any of the following, you will definitely want to soak in Richard Simmons' soul-probing *The True Measure of a Man*: You are weary, you've lost your way, or never found it. You've been humbled, had all the props knocked out, and been turned upside down. You want to know how you got off track, get your bearings back, and figure out what really matters. You want to surrender to the truth, and you're tired of living a lie. However, if you still think you're smarter than everyone else, you just wouldn't get it. This is a book I plan to read again."
—*Patrick Morley, PhD, author of* The Man in the Mirror *and* How to Survive the Economic Meltdown

"*The True Measure of a Man* is a book I wish I had written, which is about the best compliment I can pay to any book. It is what I would call a great read—both accessible and profound in its understanding of the inner forces that make up the male psychology as a man passes through midlife into, hopefully, a productive and fulfilling second season."
—*Bob Buford, Founder and Chairman, Leadership Network, author of* Halftime *and* Finishing Well

"*The True Measure of a Man* is a book for every man of every faith or no faith at all. He'll learn why he doesn't have to live with the guilt, insecurity, and fear that most men experience but often pretend they don't."
—*Fred Barnes, Executive Editor,* Weekly Standard, *and regular contributor/commentator with* FOX News Channel

D0465558

"As a coach, I've always had a desire to help shape the character of young players. Later, that burden extended to men in general through Promise Keepers. *The True Measure of a Man* captures the importance of character over achievement. He connects the dots for men who are looking for something more in their lives than mere success. I recommend this book for men at any stage of their lives."
—*Coach Bill McCartney, founder of Promise Keepers, author of* Two Minute Warning

"Richard E. Simmons III's book *The True Measure of a Man* is so full of common sense and practicality. It is especially poignant and meaningful at such a critical time in our country. May we all come to know God's grace, that he might teach us humility and kindness for all."
—*Ben Crenshaw, golf legend and two-time Masters Tournament winner*

"*The True Measure of a Man* is a provocative and credible challenge to the conventional wisdom of modern man's value system. Richard Simmons gives us a clear picture of how we deceive ourselves into a false reliance on our own accomplishments to establish our identity and our worth. And he wisely counsels that we are in treacherous territory! Thankfully, he gives explicit guidance to a liberating and transformational course for a hopeful and fulfilling life. This is an inspirational and uplifting work!"
—*Claude B. Nielsen, Chairman and CEO, Coca-Cola Bottling Co. United*

"Richard Simmons' book *The True Measure of a Man* provides inspirational and powerful answers to so many of the challenges men

face in today's world. He helps men better understand the forces that drive them and provides a framework for us to deal with issues we cannot and should not avoid. Ultimately, he provides us with a vision of the type of men we can become! Simmons' timeless wisdom is a must read and should be shared from generation to generation."
—*Lee Styslinger III, President and CEO of Altec, Inc.*

"Life inevitably presents us with difficult challenges, often as a consequence of the unhealthy and unrealistic expectations we impose upon ourselves and others . . . Richard Simmons' *The True Measure of a Man* vividly presents the tensions and traps each of us must confront on a recurring basis and masterfully teaches what truly matters. It makes for compelling reading—so much so that I read it twice."
—*W. Stancil Starnes, Chairman and CEO, ProAssurance Corp.*

"Richard's book *The True Measure of a Man* provides answers to men's deepest questions and helps them understand what they are feeling as they go through the storms of life. He points us to a life of contentment that can only be found in the Lord. I believe every man should read this book."
—*Pat Sullivan, Heisman Trophy winner, head football coach, Samford Univ.*

"Richard Simmons knows the hearts and speaks the language of today's business leaders. His message of God's lovingkindness and our need for self-examination, purpose, and contentment is profound. It is a timeless message but an all the more compelling one during these challenging times."
—*Dr. Rob Pearigen, President, Millsaps College*

"*The True Measure of a Man* is a timely book. I have seen many men go through difficult times these last few years. I believe one of the most critical needs for a man in times of economic distress is wisdom. Richard provides powerful insight into how to respond to the storms of life, and where a man should get his true identity. It is a very meaningful book!"
—*Miller Gorrie, Chairman and CEO, Brasfield & Gorrie Construction*

"In *The True Measure of a Man,* Richard Simmons gathers a wide variety of compelling stories, illustrations, quotes, and scriptures, and he delivers a timeless message that men desperately need to hear."
—*Danny Wuerffel, Heisman Trophy winner*

"Richard Simmons knows men and he knows the gospel. *The True Measure of a Man* is a masterful presentation of the truth of the gospel to us men who are all too prone to seek our identity in affluence and accomplishment rather than Jesus Christ. Simmons shows with compelling insight that the call of Christ provides the true measure of every man."
—*Drayton Nabers Jr., former Chief Justice of the Alabama Supreme Court*

"Most every male has been told throughout his life to 'be a man.' Today's vernacular says, 'man up!' But most people have no concept of what that means. Richard Simmons addresses the issue of how to measure our manhood. He helps us discover in a clear and powerful way what makes us feel like a man, look like a man, and be a real man. You will be empowered to experience joy and contentment as you read *The True Measure of a Man.*"
—*Dr. Cliff Self, Man UP Ministries, author of* Man UP, Release the Champion in You

"Richard Simmons has inspired me and my Christian walk for many years. I was anxious to read his book *The True Measure of a Man* and enjoyed it immensely. It cuts right to the heart of what is truly important in life. As we all strive to live successful lives, Richard's message about living a life of significance was inspiring for me."

—*Joe Dean Jr., Athletics Director, Birmingham-Southern College*

"This is a great book for men, especially those who want to understand what drives them to succeed. It is truly a book that positively impacted my life."

—*Joey Jones, head football coach, the University of South Alabama*

"There have been many books written about success. Success, like wealth, has many definitions. The best way to measure success is on a personal level. Richard Simmons' book *The True Measure of a Man* challenges us to enter into a more personal relationship with Jesus Christ. As you read this book, no matter where you are in your walk with the Lord, it stirs up a desire to love Him more—to truly know Him. This is must reading for this season."

—*Heeth Varnedoe III, retired president and COO of Flowers Foods*

"There is an old Appalachian saying that is derived from a folk game. If you have done very well, you have 'shaken the rag off the bush.' Richard Simmons has shaken the rag with *The True Measure of a Man*. This work is so full of practical insights about life and death, it should be distributed, like an owner's manual, to all men over thirty."

—*Barry M. Buxton, President, Lees-McRae College*

"This is an amazing book! I highly recommend it to all men."
—*Jay Barker, former professional football player, radio sports commentator*

"Richard Simmons' *The True Measure of a Man* is an honest and transparent look at men and the ever changing, swirling landscape of men's issues that surround our lives. The book embraces earthy and relational anecdotes that allow us to take the measure of our lives and reflect on our spiritual journey and life. Enjoy *The True Measure of a Man* and pass it on."
—*Rev. B. J. Weber, President of the New York Fellowship, and Chaplain of the New York Yankees (1991-2003)*

THE
TRUE
MEASURE
OF A
MAN

9/25/18

Also by Richard E. Simmons III

Remembering the Forgotten God

Safe Passage

The True Measure of a Man – Prison Edition

Reliable Truth

A Life of Excellence

Sex at First Sight: Understanding the Modern Hookup Culture

Wisdom: Life's Great Treasure

THE
TRUE
MEASURE
OF A
MAN

How Perceptions of Success,
Achievement & Recognition Fail
Men in Difficult Times

RICHARD E. SIMMONS III

UNION HILL
PUBLISHING

Birmingham, Alabama

The True Measure of a Man
by Richard E. Simmons III

Unless otherwise identified, Scripture verses have been taken from: the
New American Standard Bible, Copyright © 1960, 1963, 1968, 1971,
1973, 1975, 1977 by The Lockman Foundation. Verses marked NLT are
taken from the Holy Bible, New Living Translation, Copyright © 1996.
Used by permission of Tyndale House Publishers, Inc., Wheaton, IL
60189.

ISBN 978-1-939358-11-0

For Worldwide Distribution
Printed in the U.S.A.

Union Hill Publishing
200 Union Hill Drive, Suite 200
Birmingham, AL 35209

www.thecenterbham.org

To Dad, my hero—

Richard E. Simmons Jr.

(3/10/28 – 11/21/08)

CONTENTS

FOREWORD

I have been speaking to men, counseling men, and teaching men for more than thirty years. I have worked with businessmen, leaders, cowboys, prisoners, athletes and coaches in the NFL, military from privates to generals, educated, dropouts, all ages, all walks of life. You know what? At the center . . . we are all the same!

Richard Simmons gets it, and he lays it out in this book better than any book I have ever read. Every man I have given this book to has read it, and then he wants to buy more to give them to his friends. Men seriously don't do that! I had a man at the University Club Washington tell me he has read it five times. I have never seen that happen! Men just *get* this book. They feel they are reading about themselves.

Here is what I hear from men all the time: They struggle with feelings of 1) insecurity, 2) inadequacy, 3) isolation, 4) loneliness, and 5) fear washed in anxiety. Why? They have the wrong set of dreams—all wrong—and they don't know who they are.

I recently read portions of Richard's book to a packed ballroom at the Hilton. It was a breakfast for business professionals. There were seven hundred in attendance. As I read Richard's words describing the true life accounts of men being tossed about by the hard realities of life, I saw the people in that ballroom sit motionless and mesmerized. It was their story, and they all knew it.

It is heartbreaking to see men waste their entire lives trying to convince other people that they are someone they are not. This is why men's souls do not grow mighty in spirit and courage. They spend their existence covering up and living in fear they will one day be discovered as a fraud. There is a voice inside them that keeps telling them that in spite of all the ornaments they collect in life, they are still not OK. The results are a lifelong tension with guilt, shame, and anxiety.

That's why this book is dynamite. Richard tells men who they really are. He gives them what they need to finally "get it." I had a general at the Pentagon tell me with a saddened passion, "Jerry, what I could have done for my men if I had only known all of this sooner!"

It has always been understood that in times of crises God expects His men to be the brave ones that others can count on. Well, we're in a crisis. Where are all the brave men?

If you desire for your arms to grow stronger and your heart to be made braver, read this book with a pen in your hand. Underline the parts that speak to your life. Cowboy up and buy some more books and get them in the hands of other men that matter to you.

For me personally, this book has been one of the great gifts I have received from the hand of God through the mind and heart of Richard Simmons.

—*Jerry Leachman, Chaplain of the Washington Redskins (1995-2007)*
September 2010
Washington, D.C.

PREFACE

The True Measure of a Man resulted when it was suggested I put together a book for men based on a series of talks I had given to large groups of businessmen in 2009. These talks focused on how hard it generally is to face the economic challenges in our lives in light of the recent economic hardship the entire world has been experiencing. The community of businessmen I speak to on such issues strongly urged me to move forward with this project.

The purpose of this book, then, is to help us men realize that if we are going to be healthy, vibrant people, we must come to terms with the reality that we are not masters of the universe. It is in our interests to admit that we do indeed have certain deficiencies and weaknesses.

In my efforts to communicate truth and wisdom to others in my speeches, I have fashioned my style after the apostle Paul when he delivered his famous speech in Athens to the pagan Greek thinkers and intellectuals (Acts 17). In order to connect with them, Paul quoted liberally from their poets and their philosophers in order that they might better understand the spiritual truth he was trying to convey.

I truly believe we are living in unprecedented times, and as we look out into the future, there is a great deal of uncertainty. Life is quite scary for many of us. As a matter of fact, there is not a man I know who is not wondering what is going to happen next and how it will impact him and his family.

We all know in our hearts that there are too many men living alone in their private worlds of self-doubt and fear. They live with a sense of powerlessness because they have come to realize that so much of what takes place out in the world is completely out of their control.

The book of Proverbs exhorts us to seek knowledge, with the understanding that the goal of knowledge is wisdom. My hope is that everyone who reads this book will better understand themselves, their fears, and the forces that drive them. My hope is this book will provide wisdom to you, the reader, to enable you to better navigate life in the future.

PART I · WHAT WILL THEY THINK OF ME?

---◆---

Forced to take a buyout from the *Kansas City Star* last summer, Paul Wenske lost his sense of identity.

"I'd been an investigative reporter all my life, and then boom," says Mr. Wenske, an award-winning journalist of 30 years. "Suddenly you're not the same person you used to be. You look in the mirror: Who are you?"
—from *The Wall Street Journal,* February 12, 2009

1

The Persona

---◆---

The true worth of a man is to be
measured by the objects he pursues.

—*Marcus Aurelius*

---◆---

I have lived most of my life around men who are affluent and
have experienced varying degrees of business success. These last
nine years, as director of the Center for Executive Leadership, I
have occupied the position of teacher, coach, and counselor to
many of them. In the process of doing my job, they have confirmed
a truth that I knew deep down to be true—an essential part of the
mystique of business success is to present a corporate happy face by
projecting an image of strength and competence to the outside
world. As a result, many men feel a huge pressure to maintain the
image that they are bulletproof, that they can handle any problem,
any struggle, at any and all times.

However, I have discovered that in any man's life, true success cannot be sustained over any extended period of time by denying the existence of internal struggles. Deeply personal issues such as identity, fear, discontentment, and depression are issues all men must deal with at some time in their lives, but generally they are at a loss as to what they should do about them.

Almost ten years ago, a man I know sent me a copy of a parable from a book by one of my favorite authors, Gordon MacDonald. In this book, *The Life God Blesses: Weathering the Storms of Life That Threaten the Soul*, MacDonald tells a modern parable about a wealthy man who wanted to build a fine yacht that would have no equal. The story, which I closely paraphrase below, is about how men establish their identities. The parable explains why we feel this great need to impress others and, in the process, how we weaken the foundations of our lives. Furthermore, it highlights just how important the foundations of our identities are if we intend to weather and survive the storms of life.

MacDonald's story so resonated with me and my understanding of men's struggles that it perfectly captures what this book, at its heart, is all about. Therefore, I thought it would be the perfect way to introduce the major themes we will look at in the course of these pages.

THE WRECK OF *The Persona*

Once a very prosperous man decided to build for himself a sailing yacht. His intention was that it would be the most talked-about boat that ever sailed. He was determined to spare no expense or effort.

As he built his craft, the man outfitted it with colorful sails, complex rigging, and comfortable conveniences in the cabin. The decks were made from teakwood; all the fittings were custom-made of polished brass. And on the stern, painted in gold letters, readable from a considerable distance, was the name of the boat, *The Persona*.

As he built *The Persona*, the man could not resist fantasizing upon the anticipated admiration and applause from club members at the launching of his new boat. In fact, the more he thought about the praise that was soon to come, the more time and attention he gave to the boat's appearance.

Now—and this seems reasonable—because no one would ever see the underside of *The Persona*, the man saw little need to be concerned about the keel, or, for that matter, anything that had to do with the issues of properly distributed weight and ballast. The boat builder was acting with the perceptions of the crowd in his mind—not the seaworthiness of the vessel. Seaworthiness seems not to be an important issue while one is in dry dock.

"Why should I spend money or time on what is out of sight? When I listen to the conversations of people at the club, I hear them praising only what they can see," he told himself. "I never remember anyone admiring the underside of a boat. Instead, I sense that my yachting colleagues really find exciting the color and shape of a boat's sails, its brass fittings, its cabin and creature comforts, decks and wood texture, potential speed, and the skill that wins the Sunday afternoon regattas."

And so, driven by such reasoning, the man built his boat. And everything that would be visible to the people soon began to gleam with excellence. But things that would be invisible when the boat entered the water were generally ignored. People did not seem to take notice of this, or if they did, they made no comment.

The builder's sorting out priorities of resources and time proved to be correct: members of the boat club did indeed understand and appreciate the sails, rigging, decks, brass, and staterooms. And what they saw, they praised. On occasion he overheard some say that his efforts to build the grandest boat in the history of the club would certainly result in his selection as commodore.

When the day came for the maiden voyage, the people of the club joined him dockside. A bottle of champagne was broken over the bow, and the moment came for the man to set sail. As the breeze filled the sails and pushed *The Persona* from the club's harbor, he stood at the helm and heard what he'd anticipated for years: the cheers and well-wishes of envious admirers who said to one another, "Our club has never seen a grander boat than this. This man will make us the talk of the yachting world." Soon *The Persona* was merely a blip on the horizon. And as it cut through the swells, its builder and owner gripped the rudder with a feeling of fierce pride. What he had accomplished! He was seized with an increasing rush of confidence that everything—the boat, his future as a boat club member (and probably as commodore), and even the ocean—was his to control.

But a few miles out to sea a storm arose. Not a hurricane—but not a squall either. There were sudden gusts in excess of forty knots and waves above fifteen feet. *The Persona* began to shudder, and water swept over the sides. Bad things began to happen, and the poise of the captain began to waiver. Perhaps the ocean wasn't his after all.

Within minutes *The Persona*'s colorful sails were in shreds, the splendid mast was splintered in pieces, and the rigging was unceremoniously draped all over the bow. The teakwood decks and the lavishly appointed cabin were awash with water. And then before the man could prepare himself, a wave bigger than anything he'd ever seen hurled down upon *The Persona*, and the boat capsized.

Now, this is important—most boats would have righted themselves after such a battering. *The Persona* did not. Why? Because its builder had ignored the importance of what was below the waterline. There was no weight there. In a moment when a well-designed keel and adequate ballast might have saved the ship, they were nowhere to be found. The man had concerned himself with the appearance of things and not enough with the needed resilience and stability in the secret, unseen places where storms are withstood.

Furthermore, because the foolish man had such confidence in his sailing abilities, he had never contemplated the possibility of a situation he could not manage. And that's why later investigations revealed that there were no rescue devices aboard: no rafts, life jackets, or emergency radios. And the result of this mixture of poor planning and blind pride was that the foolish man was lost at sea.

Only when the wreckage of *The Persona* was washed ashore

did the man's boat-club friends discover all of this.

They said, "Only a fool would design and build a boat like this, much less sail in it. A man who builds only above the waterline does not realize that he has built less than half a boat. Didn't he understand that a boat not built with storms in mind is a floating disaster waiting to happen? How absurd that we should have applauded him so enthusiastically."

The foolish man was never found. Today, when people speak of him—which is rare—they comment not upon the initial success of the man or upon the beauty of his boat, but only upon the silliness of putting out on an ocean where storms are sudden and violent. And doing it with a boat that was really never built for anything else but the vanity of its builder and the praise of spectators. It was in such conversations that the owner of *The Persona*, whose name has long been forgotten, became known as simply the foolish man.

An Unexamined Life Is Not Worth Living

I find that as I share this parable with men, it powerfully speaks into their lives. It is one of the clearest examples of how we can develop such a misguided understanding of how to measure our lives. My desire is to challenge every man to examine the way he measures his life, how he measures his success; otherwise, he may find himself in the same boat as this foolish man.

2

LIFE IS, AFTER ALL, DIFFICULT

God made man simple; man's complex
problems are of his own devising.

—*Ecclesiastes 7:29, author paraphrase*

Back in the 1970s one of the most popular and best-selling pieces of nonfiction was M. Scott Peck's book *The Road Less Traveled.* The opening line in the book was this simple statement: "Life is difficult." As I work, teach, and counsel businessmen, I think often of these words because I believe they express a simple truth. Irrespective of how talented, attractive, intelligent, or wealthy you may be, life *is* difficult and full of struggles and pain. So many people live silently with broken dreams and broken lives.

Moses' words, written thirty-five hundred years ago, confirms this reality of life in the oldest of all the Psalms:

Seventy years are given to us! Some may even reach eighty. But even the best of these years are filled with pain and trouble; soon they disappear, and we are gone (Psalm 90:10 NLT).

THE STRUGGLES IN A MAN'S LIFE

A man I have known for many years recently lamented the fact that in the last twelve months, six men in his community—men he knew or was acquainted with—had committed suicide. Over the years he had struggled himself with depression. He shared with me how men in the midst of pain and turmoil often will simply withdraw and isolate themselves from others. It is as if they are ashamed of the fact that they are going through difficult times. They somehow come to believe that "real men" should never get down or discouraged.

He then told me something that really surprised me. "In the midst of my depression, I never contemplated suicide, but there were many times I wished I were not alive."

In response to this conversation, I did some research. What I discovered was quite astounding. Of all the suicides in the United States, 80 percent are committed by men. This fact reminded me of a conversation I had a number of years ago with a man who was the executive director of a large drug and alcohol recovery center. This particular center worked with both men and women who were struggling with addictions. I had the opportunity to be the speaker several times at their chapel services, and I could not help but notice that for every one woman, there were eight or nine men in the audience. The director indicated that this was the national average. Furthermore, he went on to tell me that in almost all cases, these addictions were clearly symptoms of deeper and more troubling issues in the lives of these men.

When you look out into the marketplace, you see many men

coming and going, and to a man they appear to be doing just fine. No problems. Yet under an exterior life of confidence, there exists in almost all men a hidden life of fear, pain, and loneliness. And most of these men have no idea what they should do. Most of them live with great fear that they might one day be exposed.

Julie Scelfo, a talented journalist with the *New York Times*, wrote a very interesting article on men and depression that became the lead article in a *Newsweek* magazine issue. I want to share with you a few lines from this article because it strikes right at the heart of our struggles as men:

> Six million American men will be diagnosed with depression this year. But millions more suffer silently, unaware that their problem has a name or unwilling to seek treatment. In a confessional culture in which Americans are increasingly obsessed with their health . . . [they are] reluctant to own up to mental illness. But the facts suggest that, well, men tend not to take care of themselves and are reluctant to own up to mental illness. Although depression is emotionally crippling and has numerous medical implications—some of them deadly—many men fail to recognize the symptoms. Instead of talking about their feelings, men may mask them with alcohol, drug abuse, gambling, anger or by becoming workaholics. And even when they do realize they have a problem, men often view asking for help as an admission of weakness, a betrayal of their male identities . . . "Our definition of a successful man in this culture does not include being depressed, down or sad," says Michael Addis, chair of psychology at Clark University in Massachusetts. "In many ways it's the exact opposite. A successful man is always up, positive, in charge and in control of his emotions."

Though I deal frequently with men and their problems, I am no expert on depression; it is a very complex illness and difficult for the average person to understand. One psychiatrist shared with me that there are many factors that can contribute to depression—biological, psychological, situational, social, and spiritual factors. However, I find Scelfo's article to be quite revealing. Men view an admission that they are depressed or that they need help as a declaration of weakness, a betrayal of their male identity.

In varying degrees, I believe all men are afflicted by this phenomenon. We have been repeatedly told that on those occasions when we encounter hardship, we should just suck it up and deal with it. Real men know how to fix things, and of course, this includes all of the curves life throws at us. However, when we finally come to realize that we can no longer make the fear and pain in our lives go away, we often simply retreat. We choose to hide our true selves from others. We isolate ourselves only to find that we silently suffer. I believe retreat is the worst decision a man can make in difficult circumstances; it makes for a very lonely life.

Psychotherapist Anthony de Mello has made this observation:

> Look at your life and see how you have filled its emptiness with people. As a result they have a stranglehold on you. See how they control your behavior by their approval and disapproval. They hold the power to ease your loneliness with their company, to send your spirits soaring with their praise, to bring you down to the depths with their criticism and rejection. Take a look at yourself spending almost every waking moment of your day placating and pleasing people, whether they are living or dead. You live by their norms, conform to their standards, seek their company, desire their love, dread their ridicule, long for their applause, meekly submit to the guilt they lay upon you; you are terrified to go against the fashion in the way you dress or speak or act or even think.

In thinking through and trying to understand what is going on in the depth of a man's life, I have come to a conclusion by examining my own heart. There is one question we men are always asking

10

ourselves. It often seems to be the central question that must finally be answered before we will make certain decisions or take a definitive course of action. It is a question, I believe, that haunts many a man's life:

What will people think about me?

This question operates in my own personal life. I see how it impacts me emotionally, psychologically, and even spiritually.

IN MY OWN FRONT YARD

My son Dixon is thirteen years old. He is the only child old enough and strong enough to cut the grass. Not long ago, I arrived home from work and realized the lawn badly needed cutting. Unfortunately, Dixon had the flu. I knew it wasn't severe, only a low-grade fever; but nevertheless, I decided I would go ahead and cut the grass myself. As I was getting the lawn mower cranked up, Dixon walked out and we chatted for a minute or two. As we were talking, our next door neighbor drove up, apparently returning home from the grocery store. Dixon and I both waved to her, and then I started the lawn mower and he went back inside.

As I was cutting the grass, I noticed that my neighbor had purchased quite a few items from the store and needed several trips to unload her groceries. It suddenly dawned on me that she couldn't help but notice that I was cutting the grass, and my tall, strapping son had gone back in the house.

I began to wonder, *What is she thinking about my son? Lazy kid?* Then I realized how I must look! *I wonder what she is thinking about me as a father. She must think I'm a weak dad, a man who can't even get his son to help him cut the grass.* I stewed over this until she finished unloading her groceries and was back in her house. Hours

11

later, I asked myself again, *What must she have thought about me?* How foolish I felt.

Six or seven years ago was a time in our lives when the children were young and my wife, Holly, and I had lives that were laced with crazy and frenetic activity every day. We always seemed to be exhausted, which contributed to the stress in our lives and ultimately in our marriage. Finally, one day, Holly suggested we go together and visit a counselor. I was sure, of course, that it was unnecessary, but I consented and she arranged our first meeting.

I was to meet her at the counselor's office, which was in a large office building in our community. As I parked and stepped out of the car, a fear began to come upon me and very quickly turned into almost panic. *What will I do if I run into people I know in the parking lot or in the building? What do I tell them? What will they think about me having to go for counseling?* I had a sick feeling in my stomach.

As I entered the building, I took control of my emotions and went to the office address Holly had given me. As I approached the office suite, I opened the door only to discover that matters were far, far worse than my original concern had led me to believe. This was a large counseling practice, and I was about to enter a waiting room full of people! As I walked in, I nervously looked around and was relieved when I realized that nobody looked familiar.

We met with this counselor several times, and it proved to be invaluable for us individually and for our marriage. However, each time I approached the door to the waiting room, I could never completely shake my fear of running into someone and having to explain why I needed to see a counselor. As I look back on this time in my life, it's clear what troubled me the most—once again the question: *What will people think about me?*

I believe that all men daily ask themselves this same question in one form or another—when they are buying a new car, moving into a certain neighborhood, joining a particular country club, or choosing those with whom they will socialize. What we are really asking ourselves is, *What do people think of me as a man? Do I measure up in their eyes as they see the choices I am making?* For in today's world, life for us as men is all about what we do and how successful we are at what we do.

What we are really asking ourselves is,
*What do people think of me as a man? Do I measure up
in their eyes as they see the choices I am making?*
For in today's world, life for us as men is all
about what we do and how successful
we are at what we do.

I am always wondering, *What do they think about what I do? How do you rate what I do? What would happen to me if I fail at what I do?* As I have examined my own life, I have realized that what I really fear is the thought of experiencing shame in my life. The fear of shame paralyzed me as I cut the grass, all the while wondering what my neighbor thought about me as a father. I also feared the sense of shame I would experience were I to run into someone I knew when my wife and I went to the counselor's office.

We have come to believe that men should never display any type of weakness. We should never experience business failure. We should never be subject to emotional and psychological pain. And, of course, real men should never get depressed.

Shame, according to the popular lecturer Malcolm Smith, is

the "leukemia of masculinity." It makes so many men determined to hide their fears and their faults. If we believe we do not have what it takes to be a man—that we are not adequate and we do not measure up—it invalidates our sense of manhood. Shame is what destroys men's lives.

Finally, I am convinced one of the reasons this fear of shame is so paralyzing is because so many of us have been scarred by it from events in our past. It could be from shameful events in childhood, as a teenager, or possibly from something that happened in college. So we purpose in our hearts to never experience that type of pain again, without realizing the unintended consequences it can bring into our lives.

ONE MAN'S STRUGGLE, ANOTHER'S SALVATION

Before moving forward in this book, however, you should know that if any of the thoughts I have shared up until this point are true in your life, you are not an aberration. In fact, I would say you are in the norm. We all fear shame and when we experience it, we retreat into ourselves, trying to protect our image as strong men. We all wear masks of some kind because we are immobilized by the question that we ask ourselves should others discover our secret shame: *What are people going to think of me?*

Bill Thrall, in his book *TrueFaced*, states that eventually all our masks will crack and inevitably our true selves will be exposed. This most recent economic crisis certainly has caused the masks of many men to crack and crumble. The pain for many has been unbearable.

Thrall, however, offers us an interesting, deeper view of life's difficulties. He suggests that the struggles we face could be the best things that could ever happen to us because if our masks succeed and help us to remain hidden and protected, who would ever really know us? We would be totally inauthentic, living only to perform for and impress others. Most significantly, we might go through all our days missing out on the life God intended for us.

PART II ·FREE TO CHOOSE

When you have to make
a choice and don't make it,
that is in itself a choice.

—*William James*

3

A MAN'S IDENTITY

———————◆———————

Men lust, but they know not what for:
They fight and compete, but they forget the
prize ... they chase power and glory,
but miss the meaning of life.

—*George Gilder*

———————◆———————

Some time shortly after the economic meltdown of 2008, the *Wall Street Journal* carried two separate reports of men who had taken their lives because their businesses had failed. In the months leading up to that historic economic downturn, their businesses had been flourishing. I am sure they would have found it quite amusing if you had told them earlier that they would soon be destitute.

And though I do not know anything about their personal lives, I do know that there is something deeply perplexing and disturbing

18

that goes on in the innermost being of a man when his business, his job, or his livelihood is threatened. I recently received an email from a man who has done well in the world of business, a man I know to have a significant net worth. His words were forthright and penetrating:

> Permit me if you will to ramble about some recent discoveries I have made in my personal life. Like many in our country, I have been incredibly dismayed over the last six months about the enormous depletion of value in the stock market and the real threat of the recession waylaying my business and the businesses of many others. I have spent many anxious hours in sadness and worry over the tremendous loss of wealth and the loss of future business opportunity (at least in the short run). As a Christian, I have had to ask myself, *Why am I in such turmoil?* I have come to realize that life to me is money, affluence, and financial security. My faith has been uncovered and found to be very flimsy and really of no account in terms of my contentment.
>
> I have asked myself, *What is really so troublesome inside of me about losing financial security?* The answer has come to me recently. In truth, having to live without lots of the trappings of wealth such as travel and entertainment and security is not really the biggest issue, although this is very disappointing. The real problem and fear inside me comes because I worry that without all my wealth and privilege I will not be considered a man. My feeling of manhood is found in all the trappings of wealth.

What we have here is a picture of a man who has taken a good hard look at his life and has made an honest assessment of what he sees about himself. What he wrote strikes right at the heart of our identity as men.

A good illustration of the struggle men have with the trappings of wealth and the appearance of power can be found in Arthur Miller's Pulitzer Prize winning play, *Death of a Salesman*. In the play, Willy Loman was a salesman who had been seeking business success and financial reward all his life. One of his principal tactics was trying to impress others, always putting on the airs of a big shot.

In reality, Loman struggled with his life. His family was dysfunctional. He had never experienced any type of success in his career. In fact, even on his best days he was quite mediocre.

At the end of the play he was fired from his job and faced with the harsh reality of a life that had not turned out at all the way he had planned. He had been living a charade, attempting to present to the world an image of success. In the end, he took his life.

Just after the funeral, Loman's wife asked their son Biff, "Why did he do it, why did he take his life?"

Biff's response was, "He had the wrong dreams. All, all, wrong. And he never knew who he was."

In these lines from the play, Arthur Miller reveals what plagues so many typical modern businessmen—spending lives pursuing empty dreams, not knowing who they are and not understanding the forces that drive them. Willy Loman had no idea where or from whom he derived his significance and worth. Not being able to comprehend the fear in his life nor the stresses he confronted daily, his sense of aloneness and alienation was greatly magnified.

The fictional character of Willy Loman, like so many men in everyday life, depicts what nineteenth century American philosopher Henry David Thoreau has referred to as a life of "quiet desperation." Men so often define themselves by what they do, who they know, or what they own. And when they do so, they unwittingly set themselves up for great confusion and failure in their personal lives, particularly when a major economic storm arises.

Men so often define themselves by what they do, who they know, or what they own. And when they do so, they unwittingly set themselves up for great confusion and failure in their personal lives . . .

Confusion in Tumult

A wonderful book entitled *Season of Life* addresses the identity confusion that men experience especially in challenging times. Written by Pulitzer Prize winning author Jeffrey Marx, it follows the lives of two men who coach a high school football team. They have what some may consider a highly unusual, if not unique, approach to coaching. Neither one of these men is driven by a predominating interest of winning games; rather, to the contrary, both are clearly focused on the objective of teaching high school boys how to be men. It just so happens that, in the process, their teams win a lot of championships.

In the book there is a very interesting discussion between the author, Marx, and one of the coaches, Joe Ehrmann, who had been an All-Pro defensive tackle for the Baltimore Colts. Ehrmann explains to Marx how men's identities so often get messed up because of what he calls "false masculinity."

Ehrmann says that as young boys grow up, they are consistently told to act like men. Once they hit adolescence, this becomes quite common. The problem is that most fathers never give their sons any definition of manhood. Ehrmann says that as parents we become a big part of the problem when we demand our sons to become men, when our boys have no concept of what that means. Since most fathers have no real understanding themselves of what true masculinity looks like, why should anyone expect their sons to know what is expected of them?

Marx writes about how Coach Ehrmann often conducts men's workshops and generally begins them with a simple exercise. Each participant is handed a note card and is asked to write down his definition of the word *masculinity*. As Ehrmann puts it, "Most men are absolutely dumbfounded by the question." They have no idea how to respond and most of them leave the cards blank.

In other words, many men, who may consider themselves to be real men, are, in fact, just clueless. This is why Ehrmann believes that if young men are not taught about true masculinity at home, their lives will be shaped by the culture and the messages they receive on masculinity and manhood.

I think it's accurate to suggest this is how most of us have developed our identities. It certainly helps to explain why we each have the potential to fall into dysfunctional patterns of behavior without truly knowing that it's happening.

When all is going well and life is flourishing, men generally feel good about themselves and their identities are secure. However, when economic hardship threatens their lives and their futures, life begins to unravel.

In Chris Thurman's book *The Lies We Believe*, we are afforded a rare opportunity of a perfect example of this phenomenon by looking in on a counseling session between psychologist Thurman and an anonymous client of his who worked in the real estate business:

> "I haven't closed a deal in months," said Ted, who is a real estate salesman.
> Things were rolling along fine in his life until the real estate market went belly-up. Because he was depressed and couldn't

shake it, he came to see me.

"We keep dipping into savings to get by. That can't last forever," he moaned. He sat hunched over his knees, his hands massaging his temples.

"How does doing that [your drawing down on your family savings] feel?"

He stopped, sitting straight up. "I can't stand it. I've never been so depressed. I'm normally an 'up' kind of guy! This has never happened to me before."

"Before the real estate market went bad, how did you feel?" I asked.

He sat back in his chair. "Oh, I felt great."

"Your happiness and self-worth seem to have gone up and down with the market," I observed.

"Well . . . I guess you could put it that way."

"Okay, let's stay with that thought. You feel good about yourself when things are going well. So, does that mean you're only as worthwhile as your performance?"

"Well, I don't like looking at it *that* way." He paused.

"Is it true?"

"Yeah, I guess," he mumbled. "I mean, I know I feel a lot more worthwhile when things are going good."

We need to really think through and address what this real estate professional admitted. It seems as though our lives are of much greater value when our businesses are going well. To deal with this problem, we must ask ourselves a key question: *Does our self-worth go up and down with the market or our paychecks?*

PERFORMANCE ENVY

Our culture has an obsession with performance giving us affirmation as men. In the midst of challenging times, we all have, to some degree or other, allowed ourselves to be seduced into a fog of mixed emotions. This is when we are most likely to get personal achievement confused with our value and worth as men.

Sadly many of us have come to accept as fact that a man has only as much worth as the dollars he earns out in the marketplace. Too many men have too little time for those who don't earn as much as they do, while finding far more time for those who earn much more.

When we are brutally honest with ourselves, we realize that every man is not just susceptible to this type of thinking but likely to be drawn into it. Unfortunately such a view of life can be destructive and sometimes utterly devastating. Chris Thurman shares a vivid example of how this played out in one athlete's life:

> You may remember the story of Kathy Ormsby. Ormsby was a premed honor student at North Carolina State University. She also happened to be the collegiate record holder in the women's ten thousand meter run. The day came when she had at last achieved her dream of running in the NCAA track and field championship in Indianapolis. She was the heavily favored runner in the field.
>
> Something quite unexpected, however, happened during this race. Ormsby fell behind and couldn't seem to catch the frontrunner. In a startling move after the race, she ran off the track and out of the stadium to a nearby bridge where she jumped over the side. The forty-foot fall permanently paralyzed her from the waist down.

When we equate our worth as human beings with our individual performances, we put our identities at grave risk. Any type of perceived failure from the perspective of an ego built on such a shaky foundation can easily lead us to conclude that our lives are not worth very much.

Cultural analysts say that life has not always been this way. With almost universal agreement, they tell us that in the more traditional, family-based societies of the past, men derived their identity and meaning through family relationships. A man's status came from fulfilling a defined social role (a son, a husband, a father). Work—a discipline that creates tremendous value within any social order—was not nearly as important as the fabric of one's relationships. In the traditional social order, work was seen as merely a functional means of providing for the family and improving the quality of life within the community. Work did not define a man's life's worth and value in an absolute sense as it so frequently appears to do in our modern society.

Tim Keller, a minister in New York City, goes so far as to suggest that "we are the first culture in history where men define themselves solely by performing and achieving in the workplace. It is the way you become somebody and feel good about your life." Keller adds that he believes "there has never been more psychological, social, and emotional pressure in the marketplace than there is at this very moment."

When we find our identity, our sense of worth, from someone outside of ourselves, we allow them to participate in the shaping of our identities. Once we conform to the standards of this audience, we let them determine how well we are doing in our assigned role and define how successful we are in life.

I readily admit there is an audience out there that powerfully influences who I am and how I measure up. The same is true for most men. And though we may not like it, we yearn for their approval. We want to exceed their expectations. Doesn't this beg the question: *Who is my audience, the people that I have empowered to determine my value and worth as an individual?*

Charles Cooley, a prominent and highly respected sociologist who lived from 1864 to 1929, came up with a landmark concept called the "looking-glass self," a human development theory which remains valid today. In its simplest form, the theory states:

> A person gets his identity in life based on how the most important person in his life sees him.

For a child, of course, it is the parent. We all know how important it is for parents to encourage and build up their children because we have such an impact on their sense of worth as they develop. However, as the child grows up and becomes a teenager, the parents inevitably discover they are no longer their child's number one audience. Most parents, for better or for worse, have been almost completely replaced by the child's peer group. Most teenagers value their peers' opinions more than anything else. Few of us adults would argue that peer pressure is not the most powerful force in the life of a teenager.

For an adult, particularly an adult out in the workplace, the opinion valued the most will typically come from a colleague or peer. We greatly value what other men and women in the workplace and in the community think of us. They are our audience, and we perform for them. We yearn to hear their applause.

And, sadly, whether we are a teenager or an adult, we often unconsciously allow our audience to make the final verdict on the value of our lives. The reality, however, is that the verdict is not "in" because our performance is never "over." No matter how much applause we received yesterday, we can't be certain we will receive it again tomorrow.

In essence, what I see happening in the marketplace is that many businessmen and professionals who have performed well all their lives and who have experienced incredible success now find themselves overwhelmed in the wake of an economic tsunami.

Many of these men are, for the very first time, beginning to realize that the applause of their audience is fleeting. And very few of these men in trouble seem to know what to do about it.

HOW DID WE GET HERE?

As we have seen, our postmodern society is unique in that most men define themselves today solely by their performance and their achievements in the workplace rather than relationships. Why is our culture unique? When you consider all the civilizations that have come before us, what has caused such a radical change in man's perspective?

One hundred years ago, the United States of America was predominately a production economy. Most Americans were involved in producing goods, often by hand. We led the world in production and savings. At the end of World War II, the United States experienced an unparalleled time of optimism and prosperity. Shortly afterwards, retailing analyst Victor Lebow made this observation about the rising tide of the postwar United States economy:

> Our enormously productive economy…demands that we make consumption our way of life, that we convert the buying and use of goods into rituals, that we seek our spiritual satisfaction, our ego satisfaction, in consumption… [W]e need things consumed, burned up, replaced, and discarded at an ever-accelerating rate.

Lebow's insights about the shift from production to consumption seem to have come to pass. Today we are what most economists would describe as a consumer-driven economy. Bear in mind that it is only within the last few decades that the Consumer Confidence Index has become a major leading economic indicator in America.

Our economy is so driven by a consumer culture that many of

our government officials apparently now prefer to see us collectively as consumers rather than individually as citizens. Think of the times over the past few years when you have heard a business commentator or a stock analyst say something such as, "The key to our economic recovery is that we need to get the consumer buying again."

To make matters worse, we have not just been demoted from being a nation of citizens to a nation of consumers—we have indeed, it seems, become a nation of *conspicuous* consumers. We purchase cars, homes, and all types of items, not for their functionality but rather to make a statement on our status to an audience that we hope will be watching us. How we appear in the eyes of others has become the driving force behind most of our major purchases. As one national advertiser put it, "We tap into peoples' insecurity, into their fears that they do not measure up." Advertisers do not appeal simply to our practical, common sense but to our fears that we do not measure up.

A second reason that we are the first culture in history to define itself by achieving and performing in the workplace is what the noted historian and former Congressional Librarian Daniel Boorstin calls the "graphic revolution." It started with photography and has evolved to include the television and movie industries, the Internet and digital print media, and most recently, social networking websites such as Facebook, YouTube, and Twitter. Boorstin points out that the graphic revolution has created a new kind of power—the power to make even average people doing average things "famous." So much so, he says, that we have now become a culture focused intensely on celebrity.

In the past, fame was primarily an honor earned, the result of performing heroic deeds or of making significant contributions to the welfare of the community through inventions, the advancement of education, or industrial strength. Boorstin says that today, on the other hand, people are often considered famous simply because they have become well-known through the media. Sports stars, actors and actresses, television personalities and reality stars, and children of celebrities famous for being children of celebrities are included in this group. The power and allure of fame grows stronger and stronger every day.

Boorstin's principle concern for modern society is that we are becoming more *image* conscious and less *quality* conscious. We give celebrities and the media more and more power over our lives simply because of the images they project rather than the true values they represent. But the real question is how has this impacted us as men, particularly as it relates to how we individually respond to the challenges of this new economy?

I don't believe Boorstin is saying that the graphic revolution has changed man's legitimate desires to be successful and to contribute to society. To the contrary, I think the problem he points out and underscores for us is that the standards and measures of what constitute that success have changed.

This revolution has so transformed our culture that for many in today's society, success now has more to do with public image and the *appearance* of success than it does with the quality of our work and our character. Success today is often divorced from real substance.

What I have come to realize is that many men are no longer concerned with lives of excellence. Instead, no matter how much a man accomplishes, he does not believe he is successful unless others know about it. We now regard success as achievement *plus* proper recognition of our achievement. The recognition is what makes us feel worthwhile and that we measure up as men.

Christopher Lasch, author of *The Culture of Narcissism*, has perhaps said it best:

> [Men] would rather be envied for their material success than respected for their character.

A sobering thought.

RESOLVING THE CRISIS

So how does a man who feels trapped and diminished by the opinions of others completely reorient his identity? As businessmen and high-achieving professionals, how can we reorient our identities so that economic hardship does not shatter and devastate our lives and the lives of those we love? How do we regain our bearings and solve our identity crisis?

Clearly it must start by admitting to ourselves that, like Willy Loman in *Death of a Salesman*, we have in some measure built our identity on how well we perform and how well we have won the approval of others. We must recognize that, to varying degrees, we have propped up our self-esteem and our feelings of worth and value on our achievements and the opinions of others.

How very hard it is for men to look this reality in the eye! To revisit this central, defining issue can be next to impossible for some; however, I contend every man must squarely face the difficult but inevitable truth that something may be terribly wrong in the formation of his identity, and that, yes, it starts by acknowledging the uncomfortable truth that something may be wrong with his self-image.

Tim Keller has a great illustration that points this out. He asks, "Have you ever noticed that you never think about your toes?" Of course, we never notice our toes until something goes wrong with them. When's the last time you said to yourself, "Man, my toes feel great"? When toes function as toes are meant to function, you just don't pay attention to them at all!

An unusual line of thought, perhaps, but Keller uses it to great effect as an example showing how something must be terribly wrong with most men's identities—their egos—because they seem to be always focused on them. Many a man's first question when making decisions is usually, *How does it affect me in the eyes of others?* Their second question? *What will they think of me and will I win their approval?*

Always looking to impress, egos easily become swollen with attention and the need to be noticed. Keller puts it this way:

> The ego is constantly drawing attention to itself. If your identity was healthy, like your toes, you would never notice it.

When all is said and done, we must accept that we have a radically unstable, temporal foundation on which we have anchored our identity and that something is fundamentally wrong with this approach to life.

REMEMBERED FOR WHAT, EXACTLY?

A second, related thought I would ask you to consider is the issue of legacy. Ask yourself the question, *How will my life be remembered once it is over?* St. Augustine wrote that thinking and reflecting on legacy is so important because it helps us think maturely about life. It helps us to reflect and reconsider who it is that we most desire to please. Jill Carattini, an editor and writer with Ravi Zacharias Ministries in Atlanta, Georgia, writes of how this worked in the life of Alfred Nobel:

Swedish chemist Alfred Bernhard Nobel was largely known as a maker and inventor of explosives. In 1866 Nobel invented dynamite, which earned him both fame and the majority of his wealth. At one point in his life he held more than 350 patents, operated labs in twenty countries, and had more than ninety factories manufacturing explosives and ammunition. Yet today he is most often remembered as the man behind the Nobel Prize, the most highly regarded of international awards for efforts in peace, chemistry, physics, literature, and economics.

In 1888 a bizarre incident occurred, which seemed to have afforded Nobel an unlikely opportunity for reflection. When Alfred Nobel's brother Ludwig died while staying in Cannes, France, the French newspapers mistakenly confused the two brothers and reported the death of the inventor of explosives. One paper's headline read brusquely: *Le marchand de la mort est mort*—the merchant of death is dead.

This incident had a significant effect on Nobel as he reflected on what his life was all about and how he would be remembered at his death. Jill Carattini beautifully concludes in her essay, "The headlines we write on earth are printed on pages that will eventually fade and crumble." Most believe this was the event that ultimately led to his establishment of the Nobel Prize and the subsequent change in his reputation.

I do not think we realize how the issue of legacy can change the course of our lives if we are only willing to step back and ask two related questions: *How do I want to be remembered?* and *What do I want my life to have been about once it is over?* Peter Drucker said that thinking about his legacy early in life is what shaped him so profoundly as an adult:

> When I was thirteen, I had an inspiring teacher of religion, who one day went right through the class of boys asking each one, "What do you want to be remembered for?" None of us, of course, could give an answer. So, he chuckled and said, "I didn't

expect you to be able to answer it. But if you can't answer it by the time you're fifty, you will have wasted your life." We eventually had a sixtieth reunion of that high school class. Most of us were still alive, but we hadn't seen each other since we graduated, and so the talk at first was a little stilted. Then one of the fellows asked, "Do you remember Father Pfliegler and that question?" We all remembered it. And each one said it had made all the difference to him, although they didn't really understand that until they were in their forties.

I'm always asking that question: What do you want to be remembered for? It is a question that induces you to renew yourself, because it pushes you to see yourself as a different person—the person you can become.

Once it finally dawns on us that we will not be remembered for what we have accomplished or what we have achieved or how much money we have made, we acquire the ability to change in a fundamental way.

Drucker is saying that once we begin to reflect on how we want to be remembered, it will impact our entire perspective. As we begin to focus on the type of people we are becoming and how our lives are contributing to the lives of others, it will change the way we measure our lives as men. Once it finally dawns on us that we will not be remembered for what we have accomplished or what we have achieved or how much money we have made, we acquire the ability to change in a fundamental way. I think this is what enabled Drucker to turn down Goldman Sachs when he was offered the position to become their chief economist. It was a position that would have paid him a huge salary and thrust him into the international limelight to new heights of fame and glory. But Drucker had a very healthy identity—he knew what he wanted his life to be about, and so he turned them down.

We must first acknowledge that we each have, to varying degrees, an unstable identity that has been built and shaped by years of performance. Then, and only then, we must step back and begin to think seriously about what we want our legacy to be in this life. And finally, if we truly want to be delivered from this addiction to perform and impress, we must discover a new audience.

THE PERSON YOU CAN BECOME

Remember earlier when we saw how all of us, in some measure or another, get our identity from someone outside of ourselves? To compound the problem we are always on the lookout for ways to please and impress these people because their opinions are what validates us.

What would happen if we let the person who determines our worth be God?

Recognizing that God is the supreme and ultimate reality who stands behind all of life is crucial for all of us. Scripture is clear about this truth. We are told in Psalm 139:16:

All the days ordained for me were written in your book before one of them came to be (author paraphrase).

In Ephesians 2:10 we learn:

We are His workmanship, created in Christ Jesus for good works, which God prepared ahead of time so that we should walk in them (author paraphrase).

Workmanship, as used by Paul here, comes from the Greek word *poiema*, which literally means "work of art." As men, our lives are of incredible value simply because we are God's work of art, His masterpiece. That alone is the marvel of life itself.

Your worth as a person has to do with your value. Your value is not based on what you do but on who made you. God is telling us that He is the One who gave us our existence, our very being. We are here for a reason, for a purpose. God has a plan for our lives—a plan that is full of meaning and purpose.

Why will people pay millions for a painting by Rembrandt? It's probably not so much because of its beauty but because of the artist who painted it. Our lives are of such great worth because each of us is God's work of art. The great demonstration of our incredible worth and value to God is that He sent His Son, Jesus, into the world. His willingness to die for us was the most visible way that God could express to each of us that we matter to Him and He loves us individually, each and every one of us. When a man can get this truth into his life it will transform his identity.

Remember what Charles Cooley said in his theory about the looking-glass self:

> A person gets his identity in life based on how the most important person in his life sees him.

What do you think would happen to a person's life if Jesus Christ were the most important person in that person's life? What if Jesus Christ were the audience we sought to please most? It would truly transform our lives because Jesus understands we are each of incredible value. We are of infinite worth to Him. He loves us with an everlasting love.

THE MARVEL OF LIFE ITSELF

I heard a lecture by author Donald Miller given to a sizeable group of students at Harvard. He was addressing some of the same issues we have been considering. Here's what he said:

> Human beings are wired so that they need some great authority outside themselves to tell him or her who they really are. But for many people that voice is not there, because their lives are not oriented towards God. When that is the case, the very first thing that will happen in their lives will be to question their worth and their value. Does my life really matter? And this is what causes us to begin to hide ourselves from others.

Miller goes on to say that he recognizes this to be true in the lives of all people, including important people and famous celebrities. Once he saw how we no longer look to God to give us our worth and identity, he understood why we are so addicted to the approval of others and being seen as successful in their eyes.

Most of my adult life, I have been fascinated by the color and content of C. S. Lewis' writing. But in the past few years I have read several books about his personal life, and I have to say I am even more impressed with the quality of his life. It is worthwhile to consider the life of a man who was truly grounded. He was an amazing man.

"Lewis understood his true identity," says Dr. Armand Nicholi Jr., a psychiatrist at Harvard Medical School, who has studied Lewis' life extensively. In his book, *The Question of God*, Nicholi reveals why C. S. Lewis had such a healthy identity. Lewis had been an atheist for more than thirty years, then became a theist, and then a Christian. Nicholi tells us:

> As Lewis began to read the Old and New Testaments seriously, he noted a new method of establishing his identity, of coming to

terms with his "real personality." This process, Lewis writes, involves losing yourself in your relationship to the Creator. "Until you have given yourself up to Him," Lewis writes, "you will not have a real self."

Therein lies the solution to finding our true identity as men. What Lewis recognized is that if you are really going to find your life and live it to the fullest, you have to give up your life and surrender it to Christ.

Pastor and author Tony Campolo believes this paradox is the key to eliminating all the confusion in your life. Every bit of it. It is in our commitment to Christ—and the plans He has for each of us, individually—where we will truly discover who we are and what our lives are all about. The marvel of life itself.

CHOOSING THE GOD YOU WOULD SERVE

So, when all is said and done, what does it really mean to be successful, to lead a successful life? Or, to ask the question from an altogether different perspective, what if a highly competent, talented man loses his job or his business folds due to circumstances he has no control over? Is he a failure?

What if a man never reaches as high up the corporate ladder as he once aspired, nor accumulates the type of wealth he always expected? What happens to a man when he begins to realize that his life will never turn out the way he had always hoped, never to be included in the circles of the social elite or the well-connected?

What does all this really mean and what does it do to a man once he is confronted with this reality? C. S. Lewis has given us wonderful insight into these questions in a renowned speech he delivered to the students of Kings College at the University of London. He titled his speech "The Inner Ring." As he addressed the students, he warned them of the natural human desire to always want to be a part of the correct inner circles. He explained that these inner circles, these cliques, will inevitably form and re-form, in constant change throughout the seasons of a person's life. They provide no real stability.

He cautioned these students about the consuming ambition to be an insider, cozying up to those who are important and well-to-do in order to be part of an imagined elite. In doing so, Lewis says, we become like the weary traveler in the desert that chases a mirage. Ultimately, our quest to be in the inner circle of the powerful will one day break our hearts.

This is the choice we all face. We can continue to allow this mortal world to define who we are and what our lives are worth, with the knowledge that one day the world will invariably break our hearts. Or alternatively, we can break the world's hold on our lives by relinquishing ourselves and our identities to become absolutely grounded in Christ's love and His commitment to our well-being. Make no mistake: irrespective of our station in life, it is a choice we all have to make that will make or break us as men.

As you read and study both the Old and New Testaments, you will notice that God is always confronting His people with a choice. I am reminded of Joshua in a pivotal moment in Israel's history when he asked the people to choose the god that they would serve. I believe that if he stood before us today, in the midst of the difficult times we are in, he would confront us with a similar choice.

Choose for yourselves today the god whom you will serve: the god of wealth, the god of prestige and power, the god of pleasure, the god of achievement. But as for me and my family, we will serve the Lord (Joshua 24:15, author paraphrase).

A Man's Identity

Each of us must choose the god we are going to serve, and then we will have to live with all the consequences that flow from that choice.

4

A Man's Courage

--- ❖ ---

We all have a basic motivational drive,
every human heart has something that drives
them. It gets us through life. It moves us to do
what we do. And for most of us, I believe,
it is fear. —*Tim Keller*

--- ❖ ---

Warren Buffett's annual letter to the shareholders of Berkshire Hathaway in late February 2009 clearly reflected his thoughts on how this current economic environment impacts our lives as men:

> By the fourth quarter of last year, "the credit crisis coupled with tumbling home and stock prices, had produced a paralyzing fear that engulfed the country," Buffett said.
> "A freefall in business activity ensued, accelerating at a pace that I have never before witnessed. The U.S.—and much of the world—became trapped in a vicious negative feedback cycle.

Fear led to business contraction, and that in turn led to even greater fear."

It is important to note he used the word *fear* three times— most notably when he states that the credit crisis that began in the fall of 2008 "has produced a paralyzing fear that engulfed the country."

THE FEAR ITSELF

When people ask me what I see going on in men's lives in my community, my answer is very simple: fear. A very prominent man in Alabama, who apparently has experienced financial success most of his life, recently remarked, "For the first time in my life, I am really afraid."

Simply stated, fear is created by uncertainty over the future, even if the ultimate outcome has only the slightest potential to be negative. Fear can produce a complexity of emotions. It can be a powerful force for taking positive action in our lives, or it can produce potentially crippling emotions.

Our fear is generally nothing more than living out the future before it arrives and taking steps to avoid the negative outcomes we imagine are likely to occur. The difficulty arises when these imagined negative events become greatly intensified in the realms of our imaginations. Our fear begins to worry us to death.

The word *worry* comes from an Old English word meaning to choke or to strangle. What I have seen so often is that fear and worry can indeed strangle the mind's ability to reason and think clearly. We bury ourselves in present imaginings when we worry about future events. Most men do not know how to deal with fear; they let it run wild in their minds, crippling them in a multitude of ways.

Noted historian Wayne Flynt, who has studied the Great Depression and other economic downturns in great detail, has made this observation about the times we have recently been through:

> In times like this, the real damage may not be economic, but in its human toll, which can last for generations. The stress is just incredible.

What is the human toll he speaks of? Divorce, excessive drinking, sleeplessness, anger, depression, and suicide are all a result of fear. However, I am not certain that most men know what it is they actually fear during these times of economic turmoil and over-stimulated, reckless imaginations. It is worth our consideration.

The prominent psychologist Dr. Larry Crabb says that we have two basic psychological needs in our lives—the need for *security* and the need for *significance*. What has happened is that this current economic recession—particularly the severity of it—has converged in such a way that the ability to meet both of these psychological needs has been threatened.

The result is a paralyzing fear.

SECURITY AND SIGNIFICANCE

Crabb has long maintained (as well as others, such as, most recently, Ron Blue and Jeremy White in their book *Surviving the Financial Meltdown*) that in periods of economic uncertainty:

- Women's *security* feels threatened. They worry that the mortgage won't be paid, and their children won't have food and caring.
- Men's fears, on the other hand, go much deeper. Their *significance* is threatened.

As men, just what is this psychological need we have for significance? Significance is the belief that your life makes a lasting difference. No man wants to get to the end of his life and believe that his earthly existence was not important in some way. The Danish philosopher Soren Kierkegaard put it like this: "Every person must find some way to justify their existence."

What are the ways and means men call on to stave off the universal fear that their lives are not worth anything? Tennessee Williams is considered by many to be America's greatest playwright. His plays reveal a keen insight into the human heart. One of my favorite plays (also made into an acclaimed movie in 1958, starring Paul Newman and Elizabeth Taylor) was his Pulitzer Prize winning play *Cat on a Hot Tin Roof*.

This story involves the history of a troubled wealthy family, who live on a large country estate in Mississippi. The patriarch of the family is an older, intimidating man whom they call Big Daddy. Brick, one of his two sons, is an aging football hero who struggles with alcohol. He is married to Maggie, who goes by the name of Cat. Brick and Maggie, who are childless, have a turbulent relationship primarily because of Brick's neglect of her. However, Brick goes even further to infuriate Maggie by conspicuously ignoring his brother's ambitions to gain control of the family's fortune.

At the end of the movie version, Big Daddy learns that he does not have long to live. He and Brick have a pointed exchange wherein Big Daddy describes to Brick the tension that exists between gaining wealth and finding a lifetime of significance:

> I am worth 10 million dollars in cash and blue chip stocks, but there is only one thing you can't buy on any market on earth, and that's your life when you know it is finished . . . The human animal is a beast that must eventually die, and if he has money,

he buys and he buys and he buys, and he hopes one of the things
he buys is life everlasting.

Clearly, the life everlasting that Big Daddy refers to is not to
be taken in a spiritual sense but rather as his desire that his earthly
life would have some type of permanence. He did not want to be
forgotten. Brick asks Big Daddy why he so desperately wants
grandkids. The answer is revealing:

> I want a part of me to keep on living. I won't have my life end at
> the grave.

At the end of his life, Big Daddy has realized that the wealth
he had accumulated over the course of a lifetime could never purchase what he most desired: significance.

In a commencement address the famous presidential biographer Doris Kearns Goodwin captured this same truth when
speaking of President Lyndon B. Johnson:

> A month before he died, he spoke to me with immense sadness
> in his voice. He said he was watching the American people ab-
> sorbed in a new president, forgetting him, forgetting even the
> great civil rights laws that he had passed. He was beginning to
> think his quest for immortality had been in vain, that perhaps he
> would have been better off focusing his time and attention on his
> wife and his children, so then he could have had a different sort
> of immortality through his children and their children in turn.
> He could have depended on them in a way he couldn't depend
> on the American people. But it was too late. Four weeks later he
> was dead. Despite all his money and power he was completely
> alone when he died, his ultimate terror realized.

It is hard to believe a man could achieve the office of what is arguably the most powerful leader in the world and not feel like his life has had much enduring value. But, there it is.

RECKLESS IMAGININGS

When we let our imaginations run wild, we soon find that our thoughts become focused on all types of imagined repercussions and consequences. Such reckless imaginings based on unrealistic fears creates a false reality of the future that begins to appear so very real, almost inevitable. Without exercising caution and restraint, these imaginings soon will cascade into all other areas of our lives, affecting our judgment and our relationships as it did for President Johnson.

I believe this search for significance is one of the chief explanations for why most men are haunted by the prospect of failing, particularly failing in front of the people in their community. Tim Keller, after all his years as a pastor to men in New York City, has found that gaining or losing significance is clearly one of the basic motivational drives in the lives of men. He says the thought of failure to most men is such a nightmare that it can be equated only to a kind of psychological death. For this reason, I truly believe most men are not driven to succeed; on the contrary, they are driven *not to fail*.

As we noted in the book's early pages, fear and shame are a primary cause of depression in men during times of trouble. Too few men know how to share with others their fears, the pain in their lives, and their struggles, particularly if it makes them look weak or like a failure. So men naturally clam up and silently carry the load on their backs. In the process they withdraw from others and live very lonely, isolated lives.

This withdrawal, of course, has a significant impact on our relationships with other men because what we really fear is how our failure will appear in the eyes of our peers and especially those we consider our friends. This explains why we always try to maintain the appearance that our lives are flourishing and that we really have it together but have no lifelong deep relationships. If all I can offer you is a superficial image of my true self, why should I expect to end up with anything but superficial relationships that have no real depth? Fear of failure and our inability to deal with that fear create shallow personal relationships.

The fear of failure also causes individuals to play it safe in life. We find ourselves avoiding reasonable risks that we should probably take. Not wanting to look bad in the eyes of others, our judgment becomes critically impaired, and we find ourselves not pursuing viable opportunities—even when failure is a remote possibility. Larry Crabb says that men try to arrange their lives so that everything is predictable and under their control. They pursue endeavors where they feel competent and can hide their inadequacies, avoiding what they fear and thereby creating a feeling of safety.

The real problem with this approach to life is that a man most likely will never reach his full potential. By playing it safe and refusing to expose himself to failure, he will find himself later in life asking the question, *What if?*

Tony Campolo tells of a study done a number of years ago by a group of sociologists. They interviewed a large number of people, and the only criteria to be chosen for the study was that you had to be at least ninety-five years old. They were asked this one question: If you could live your life over again, what would you do differently? One of the most common answers of this group of elderly people was, "If I could go back and live my life over again, I would have taken more risks."

What strikes me with this answer is that these people in their twilight years realized what a mistake it was to play it safe over the course of their lives because they were afraid to fail. If you think about it, most of the great accomplishments in life are the result of people willing to step out of their comfort zones into the unknown, knowing that failure is a possibility.

As men of honor and integrity, we should always be inspired and encouraged by these words of Theodore Roosevelt:

> It is not the critic who counts; not the man who points out how the strong man stumbles, or where the doers of deeds could have done them better. The credit belongs to the man who is actually in the arena, whose face is marred by dust and sweat and blood; who strives valiantly; who errs, and comes short again and again, because there is no effort without error and shortcoming; but who does actually strive to do the deeds; who knows the great enthusiasms, the great devotions; who spends himself in a worthy cause; who at the best knows in the end the triumph of high achievement, and who at the worst, if he fails, at least fails while daring greatly, so that his place shall never be with those cold and timid souls who know neither victory nor defeat.

DO YOU WANT TO GET WELL?

In the fifth chapter of the book of John, Jesus encountered a crippled man in Bethesda, and asked him an unusual question: "Do you want to get well?"

Though we might not be physically afflicted like this man, we all are afflicted in our hearts and souls. But do we want to get well? Many men will answer with a resounding no, such as the man who once told me, "I believe what you are telling me is true, but I want to stay on the path I'm on."

Let's look at Jesus' question, "Do you want to get well?" We will approach it from an altogether different perspective, a new paradigm for us to consider. Let's start by considering our current economic crisis from a biblical perspective and not just a personal, human point of view.

Several years ago, I noticed that the word *beware* popped up frequently in my readings of the Old and New Testaments. We should not be surprised that God consistently warns His people about issues that have the potential to corrupt their lives. However, what is interesting is that Jesus used the word beware primarily to warn us about believing what is false. He recognized that false teaching can lead us down the path of destruction.

The eminent Christian philosopher Blaise Pascal has said the primary reason people struggle so much in life is because they have false ideas about reality. He says it is crucial to uproot these false ideas and replace them with wisdom and truth. I wonder how many of us have false ideas about being successful, about masculinity, about what in fact is the true measure of a man.

And I wonder how many of us have false ideas about the storms we face in life. Read these significant verses that contrasts God's perspective with our very limited perspective as humans:

"For my thoughts are not your thoughts,
Nor are your ways My ways," declares the Lord.
"For as the heavens are higher than the earth,
So are My ways higher than your ways,
And My thoughts than your thoughts" (Isaiah 55:8-9).

We also read in Psalm 50:21 where God makes a very clear assertion: "You thought I was like you but I am not" (author paraphrase).

In this picture of God's infinite majesty, He is declaring to us that He doesn't think as we think nor see life as we see it. He does not see an economic crisis as you see it nor as I see it. His ways and purposes are so much higher than ours.

This contrast is particularly easy to grasp when we consider that God's perspective on time is so different from ours. It is God's view of human affairs from an eternal frame of reference that we should seek to understand. As we concentrate on God's eternal truths, we will grow to a deeper appreciation of what we already know—that our lives are but a passing moment in time.

Most of us are desperately hoping things will turn around soon. Our thoughts of prosperity and happiness are often interrupted these days by fear, especially when we turn our focus toward retirement, which looms large for many of us in the next five, ten, or twenty years. But, interestingly, in 2 Peter 3:8 we are told that one thousand years are like a day to God. We get so focused on the next few years while God's time horizon is eternal. He cares about our eternal well-being. He sees what we don't see. His thoughts and plans are so much higher than ours.

Now I want to take just a minute to reflect on a truth that we generally never consider during difficult times. I believe this truth is so crucial to grasp as we approach our fears and as we remind ourselves that God's ways and plans are so much higher and grander than ours.

THE MATURING OF THE SOUL

Imagine the horror of a Nazi concentration camp in Hungary. Imagine that we are Jews held against our will and forced to work in a factory that supplies the Nazis' growing war machine. We are just barely surviving. One day, Allied aircraft blast the area and destroy the hated factory. The next morning several hundred of us are herded to one end of the charred remains. Expecting orders to begin rebuilding, we are puzzled when the Nazi officer commands us to shovel sand into carts and haul it to the other end of the plant.

The next day the process is repeated in reverse. We are now ordered to move a huge pile of sand back to the other end of the compound. A mistake has been made. We say to ourselves, *stupid swine,* but a guard soon shouts, and we pick up our pace. Day after day we are forced to haul the same pile of sand from one end of the camp to the other.

Finally, one old man begins to cry uncontrollably; and the guard hauls him away. Another screams until he is beaten into silence. Then a young man who has survived three years in the camp darts away from the group. The guards shout for him to stop as he makes a run for the electrified fence. We all cry out, but it's too late; there is a blinding flash and a terrible sizzling noise as smoke rises from his smoldering flesh.

In the days that follow, dozens of the other prisoners go mad and run from their work, only to be shot by the guards or electrocuted by the fence. We overhear the commandant wryly remark that there soon will be no more need to use the crematorium.

I paraphrase the telling of the above story as it originally appeared in Charles Colson's book *Kingdoms in Conflict* to emphasize the point Colson made—if our struggles and pain seem purposeless, over time we will become dysfunctional. Our minds will snap.

If no meaning or purpose is behind the events as they unfold, life will always be bleak and hopeless, especially when pain and suffering enter our lives. Would it have made a difference if the Nazis had forced the prisoners to do the exact same work but instead the purpose of the labor was to assist in building an orphanage for Hungarian children who had lost their parents in the war? This shift in perspective underscores the concept Colson believes is so critically important to grasp: finding meaning and purpose behind what we are experiencing in life is everything.

Another starkly rendered example of the contrasts between two circumstances and the meaning behind them can be found in an observation made by Dr. Paul Brand. If a woman in love with her husband decides to spend a romantic evening with him and the evening ends with sexual intimacy, we can all agree that this is good for both the man and the woman. This type of intimacy is a wonderful way for a couple to express their love for one another.

Now, if we take this same woman and this time she is forcibly raped by a strange man, we cannot possibly imagine that there is no definable difference in the experience of such a horrific act from that of having sex with her husband. Physiologically, she experiences the same act, involving the same nerve endings. The former experience, however, is of great beauty. The latter is the worst nightmare a woman could imagine. The meaning behind what you are experiencing is everything.

Dr. Henry K. Beecher of Harvard Medical School made an interesting observation among the 215 wounded men from the Anzio beachhead in World War II:

> Only one in four soldiers with serious injuries (fractures, amputations, penetrated chests or cerebrums) asked for morphine, though it was freely available. They simply did not need help with the pain, and indeed many of them denied feeling pain at all. Beecher, an anesthesiologist, contrasted the soldiers' reactions to what he had seen in private practice, where 80 percent of patients recovering from surgical wounds begged for morphine or other narcotics.

Here you have two different groups of people suffering from the same exact injuries. The soldiers' responses to pain were impacted by the fact that their injuries carried with them a sense of meaning—a result of being involved in a significant mission for their country. They also had a sense of gratitude that they had survived. Yet the civilian patients with the same exact wounds saw their injuries as being depressing and calamitous, and thus "they begged for morphine or other narcotics."

Just hours before Jesus was taken into custody, He made this point to His disciples in John 16:21:

Whenever a woman is in labor she has pain, because her hour has come; but when she gives birth to the child, she no longer remembers the anguish because of the joy that a child has been born into the world (author paraphrase).

A mother's pain produces something with meaning, a new life, and for that reason she can even contemplate repeating the experience without fear and worry. The point I am making is so crucial to grasp. It is foundational if you are going to effectively deal with fear.

In the midst of the storms of life we will either allow what we are experiencing to influence our view of God, or we will allow our view of God to influence what we are experiencing.

In the midst of the storms of life we will either allow what we are experiencing to influence our view of God, or we will allow our view of God to influence what we are experiencing. If we can relinquish our ego's hunger for approval and can take a moment to re-examine our anxious fears through the lens of God's truth, I believe these fears will truly be transformed.

As you examine your particular circumstances, I ask you to consider that God makes eminently clear to us there *is* purpose in our pain and suffering. With the right mindset, we can find purpose behind the circumstances causing our fear. As a cancer survivor related his suffering to me:

[It is] through my battle with cancer I have come to understand that suffering is good for us. There is purpose in it. It makes you focus on what is really important.

I am reminded that Pulitzer Prize winning author Alexander Solzhenitsyn spent eight years of his life in prison for making a few disparaging remarks about Joseph Stalin. He went into prison an atheist and came out a Christian. After he was released, the first words out of his mouth were:

> I bless you prison—I bless you for being in my life—for there lying on rotting prison straw, I learned the object of life is not prosperity as I had grown up believing, but the maturing of the soul.

TRUE BLESSINGS, DISCOVERED COURAGE

I wonder how many of us, over the course of our busy lives, have given any great deal of thought to the question, *What is the object of life?* If we believe the object of life is to have comfort, pleasure, and prosperity, then we will see this current economic crisis as nothing more than a calamity. We will be fearful, bitter, and angry.

But if the object of life is indeed, as Solzhenitsyn suggests, the maturing of the soul—the transformation of our character through knowing and glorifying God—we will learn to see hardship, just as Solzhenitsyn did, as a true blessing in the development of our lives and our relationships with others.

How could Solzhenitsyn, or anyone in their right mind, say that after eight years of a prison sentence and being away from family, friends, and comfort, that the experience was a blessing? Solzhenitsyn tells us that his experiencing a harsh prison term was the only way for him to find the spiritual truth of life to which he had been blinded.

Maybe we should all give some thought to this possibility. What could we be blind to that might lead God to try and make a breakthrough in our lives? In Jeremiah 22:21 we read:

"I spoke to you in your prosperity. But you said: 'I will not listen!'
This has been your practice from your youth, that you have not obeyed
My voice."

Could this be true of us?

Some of life's most sacred truths can be learned only as we walk through our individual storms in life. We all have them. Yet all we ever seem to want is relief and comfort. We demand instant solutions, but what we fail to recognize is that although God can solve all of our problems, instant solutions are not important to Him. What is important to Him is how we respond to our struggles.

I find that so many men instinctively respond to their negative circumstances not only with fear but also with anger and bitterness. "Why me?" they ask. "This is not fair. I don't deserve this!"

Caught up in the process of cursing the realities of life, we most often discover that the pain actually continues to increase.

In *Where Is God When It Hurts?* Philip Yancey wrote about the highly influential twentieth century Swiss psychologist Paul Tournier's insight. "Only rarely are we the masters of events," he [Tournier] says, "but (along with those who help us) we are responsible for our reactions." In other words, we are accountable for the way we respond to the struggles we encounter. Tournier believed that a positive, active, creative response to one of life's challenges will develop us while a negative, angry one will only debilitate us and stunt our growth.

In fact, Tournier believed that the right response at the right moment might actually determine the course of a person's entire life. He found that quite often humans are presented with rare opportunities to develop and grow only through hardship and trial. Yancey further adds, "That, in fact, was why he [Tournier] moved away from the traditional pattern of diagnosis and treatment and began to address his patients' emotional and spiritual needs as well."

REFRESH YOUR UNDERSTANDING

Could my response to the storms that enter my life determine the future course of my life? Though we may not know what God is up to, we can be certain that there is purpose in our painful circumstances, whenever and however they occur. And when we know and recognize that there is meaning behind what we are experiencing, it will transform our pain and will enable us to relinquish our fear.

Malcolm Muggeridge was one of Great Britain's most beloved journalists. An agnostic for most of his life, Muggeridge stunned the world back in the 1960s when he announced that he had become a Christian. At the age of seventy-five, he made an interesting observation:

> Indeed, I can say with complete truthfulness that everything I have learned in my seventy-five years in this world, everything that has truly enhanced and enlightened my existence, has been through affliction and not through happiness, whether pursued or attained. In other words, if it ever were to be possible to eliminate affliction from our earthly existence . . . the result would not be to make life delectable, but to make it too banal or trivial to be endurable.

What we are currently experiencing in our economy is clearly a result of financial irresponsibility on a massive scale. It is a problem caused by human beings who are reaping from an over-leveraged economy. But what I find most interesting, as we look back in history, is that we seem to always find ways to make decisions that complicate our lives and bring financial trouble into our world; yet God is always there to redeem our negative circumstances. He uses them for our good if we will allow Him to do so.

The question remains, how is He attempting to use these trying times in our lives? What is He trying to teach us? I believe He is trying to make a spiritual breakthrough in the lives of each and every one of us. He is trying to remind us of how we continue to build our security and our significance on those things in life that can be taken away from us.

The great lesson of human history is that people are always looking for something else, anything else, to give them significance and security. For so many men in the world of business and commerce, God is not an option.

I am reminded of God's own words in the book of Jeremiah:

For My people have committed two evils: They have forsaken Me, the fountain of living waters, to make for themselves cisterns, broken cisterns, that can hold no water (Jeremiah 2:13, author paraphrase).

Notice that God is referring to religious people, for He calls them "My people." Yet they have forsaken Him, the fountain of living water, and have instead pursued a strategy they believe will enable them to capture the water that will satisfy the thirst and yearning of the soul. Unfortunately they always come up empty and the thirst remains.

The Bible speaks consistently of a thirst in the soul of every human. We may recognize it as a yearning for security and significance, but it is also a desire for purpose, meaning, and contentment. What we fail to recognize is that this thirst can only be quenched by God; thus, we are invited to come to the fountain of living water and drink.

Whoever is thirsty, let him come; and whoever wishes, let him take the free gift of the water of life (Revelation 22:17, author paraphrase).

C. S. Lewis demonstrates this truth powerfully in one of his stories in the *Chronicles of Narnia*. The Narnia books are a series of allegorical children's stories, yet they speak powerfully to the lives of adults as well. A young girl named Jill in Lewis' book *The Silver Chair* presents a wonderful representation of humanity. She is clearly consumed with herself and is convinced that she alone knows what is best for her life. She wants to have nothing to do with Aslan, the great and magnificent lion who represents Christ. Yet Jill is desperately searching for water:

> Jill grows unbearably thirsty. She can hear a stream somewhere in the forest. Driven by her thirst, she begins to look for this source of water—cautiously, because she is fearful of running into the Lion. She finds the stream, but she is paralyzed by what she sees there: Aslan, huge and golden, still as a statue but terribly alive, is sitting beside the water. She waits for a long time, wrestling with her thoughts and hoping that he'll just go away.
>
> Then Aslan says, "If you are thirsty, you may drink."
>
> Jill is startled and refuses to come closer.
>
> "Are you not thirsty?" said the Lion.
>
> "I am dying of thirst," said Jill.
>
> "Then drink," said the Lion.
>
> "May I—could I—would you mind going away while I do?" said Jill.
>
> The lion answered this only by a look and very low growl. And just as Jill gazed at its motionless hulk, she realized that she might as well have asked the whole mountain to move aside for her convenience.
>
> The delicious rippling noise of the stream was driving her near frantic.
>
> "Will you promise not to—do anything to me, if I come?"
>
> "I make no promise," said the Lion.

Jill was so thirsty now that, without noticing it, she had come a step nearer.

"Do you eat girls?" she said.

"I have swallowed up girls and boys, women and men, kings and emperors, cities and realms," said the Lion. It didn't say this as if it were boasting, nor as if it were sorry, nor as if it were angry. It just said it.

"I daren't come and drink," said Jill.

"Then you will die of thirst," said the Lion.

"Oh dear!" said Jill, coming another step nearer. "I suppose I must go and look for another stream then."

"There is no other stream," said the Lion.

So many men spend their lives looking for some other stream to finally and forever quench the thirsts of their souls. However, Jesus says there is no other stream. And He is very clear about the fact that if we do not drink from this spring—the fountain of living water—we will die.

5

A MAN'S TRUTH

◆

Here I am in the twilight years of my life,
still wondering what it is all about . . . I can tell
you this, fame and fortune is for the birds.

—Lee Iacocca

◆

Beware . . .

I noted earlier that Jesus uses the word *beware* primarily to warn us of believing what is false. Blaise Pascal recognized that life is hard and full of risks, and that so many of life's major problems result from people living with false ideas and beliefs about reality.

Scott Peck in his best-selling work *The Road Less Traveled* has said it this way:

> The less clearly we see the reality of the world, the more our minds are befuddled by falsehood, misperceptions, and illu-

59

sions—the less able we will be to determine correct courses of action: make wise decisions.

Have you ever given serious thought to the consequences of believing what is false about the way the world really works? More particularly, what would be the consequences if your beliefs about what it means to be successful and what it means to be a real man are false? How severely could false ideas be messing up your life? Too many men simply walk away from the thought that they could have it wrong.

Jesus, on two separate occasions, said, "The eye is the lamp of the body." He is referring to our perception of reality. He is revealing that if your perception of reality is rooted in the truth, your life will be full of light—and you will be a healthy and dynamic man—because you will know who you are and where you are going. You will know what has true value in life.

On the other hand, if your perception of reality is rooted in falsehood, your life will be full of darkness. You will stumble through life and fall, having no idea what the problem is. Therefore, as Jesus teaches us, it is crucial to understand that our view of life and masculinity must be rooted in the truth.

The person who has helped me the most to get a really good understanding of this is Coach Joe Ehrmann in Jeffrey Marx's book *Season of Life*. You will remember his discussion with Marx about how devastating it can be when men develop what he calls false masculinity. Ehrmann described to Marx how it develops in a man's life. He told Marx that the first component of false masculinity enters our lives in the early years at school. If you observe any playground you will notice boys playing competitive games. It always seems that the kid who is the fastest or who can pass and catch the football better than the others, is elevated above the crowd. He is generally regarded by his classmates as a little more masculine, somewhat superior to the other boys, and those who are not as athletic begin to develop a sense of inferiority. Ehrmann believes that much of a boy's value and sense of identity is built around that playground, much more so than the classroom.

I personally think the first time a young boy questions whether he really measures up is on the playground, when boys choose up teams for an athletic contest. A boy begins to wonder about his worth if he continually is chosen last.

Coach Ehrmann points out that when boys reach puberty, a second component of false masculinity rears its ugly head: sexual conquest. In the teenage years, a boy's ability to relate to and attract the opposite sex becomes a new way to validate his masculinity. Teenage boys who want to prove they are men begin to project an entirely new type of image, one that they believe will attract the girls. Most young boys dream of one day growing up to be the quarterback on the football team who dates the most beautiful girl in the school, the homecoming queen, the head cheerleader, or the most popular one.

The final component of false masculinity that Coach Ehrmann deals with becomes a factor when men hit the workplace. It is of course measured by financial success. Throughout the arc of his life, a man gets his identity from job titles and the size of his bank account. Those with the highest position and the most income are considered real men.

Author Marx shares these insights and more, gleaned from his observations during the time he spent with Coach Ehrmann. Marx ultimately captures the essence of Ehrmann's wisdom by concluding, "Joe had a catchy way of summarizing our cultural progression of false masculinity—'from ball field to bedroom to billfold.'"

In the process we find ourselves competing and comparing ourselves with all the men in our sphere of influence. Erhmann believes that this approach to life sets men up for tremendous failure. It is just a matter of time.

Just think how young boys compare their athletic ability with others, and how the teenager wants to date the most beautiful girl in the school. Then as adults we compare our homes, our cars, and our vacations with our friends in the community. We even compare our children and their accomplishments with our peers' children.

What too many good men fail to realize is that this approach to life is utter foolishness. The ball field, the bedroom, and the wallet are merely outward experiences that fail to translate into permanent inner fulfillment and contentment. Furthermore, as time goes by, the ball field, the bedroom, and the wallet are never able to convince us in our innermost being that we truly measure up as men.

THE TRUE MEASURE OF A MAN

I have reflected on this topic a great deal. In my position as director for the Center of Executive Leadership, I have seen large numbers of men over the years who wrestle with these issues. I am now in the second half of my life, and at this stage as an executive director of a nonprofit organization, I have come to certain conclusions:

- I think that most of us realize being a great athlete in our youth is really of no great value any more.
- I bet that a handful of men reading this book attracted really good-looking women when they were younger (you know who you are), but they too now realize that this doesn't really matter any more.

- I have concluded that most men who are approaching mid-life and older—particularly those whose children have left the house—find that their lives are focused on two things: what they are achieving and what they are experiencing.

ACHIEVEMENT AND EXPERIENCE

When I speak of achieving I mean:

- *In the workplace:* Securing a significant job title, managing an increasing number of people, becoming indispensable to an organization's productivity or income production.
- *As an entrepreneur:* Building and growing your own business.
- *As an investor:* Amassing a personal fortune and a high level of income, retiring at a young age.

These are the primary means by which we gain status in the community and in the eyes of others. It gives us a sense of importance. We want to be able to say with confidence, "I measure up."

When I speak of focusing on our experiences I mean:

- *The pleasures of life:* Going to your lake or beach house; participating in sporting events; dining at fine restaurants; collecting books, music, or movies.
- *Hobbies:* Hunting, golf, fishing, skiing, woodworking, spectator sports.
- *Traveling:* Europe in springtime and in fall, gaining knowledge of the world and new cultures, learning new languages and customs.

Men who live in prosperous cultures have always been in search of just such happy, pleasurable experiences. Of course, this is why money holds such importance to us. It affords a life with easy access to any number of such satisfying experiences. Money allows us to broaden our experiences with fine restaurants, lavish vacations, and expanding our hobbies.

Now in no way am I condemning achievement or pleasure or money. But I love what the fictional character in the movie based on Winston Groom's book *Forrest Gump* had to say about money:

> Now Mama said there is only so much money a man really needs, and the rest is just for showing off.

There is great wisdom here.

In one sense, I guess we could say money is a measure of achievement. It does in fact give us a reasonable scorecard to gauge added value in a complex world of business and commerce.

Moreover, if you follow the biblical principles for work (diligence; serving your client well; striving for excellence, honesty, integrity), very likely you will earn all the money you need. As for pleasure, well, pleasure is God's idea. Sensual experience can afford great delight when enjoyed within the parameters for which God designed it. But God never intended for pleasure to be able to satisfy our hearts.

When you read the Scriptures, one of the things you quickly and clearly realize is that achievement, pleasure, and the requisite material wealth to enjoy such experiences are not altogether important for their own sake in the sight of God. Such human experiences have a place, a legitimate and rightful place, of course; but God never says to pursue these with great vigor. Never are we told to pursue achievement and pleasure foremost, with all our hearts and minds.

Remember, most of God's words pertaining to money, achievement, and pleasure are words warning us of their potential corrupting influence. I think we also recognize that they do not give a person's life any great deal of meaning or purpose. Think of the car you are driving. Honestly, does it give you a real sense of satisfaction after you have driven it 25,000 miles? 50,000 miles? Why do you suddenly wake up one day and desire a new one when the old one works just fine?

I think most men rarely stop to give this much thought. Cars, boats, houses, food, sex, and hobbies do not determine the measure of a man. So, if achievement, pleasure, and money are really not that important in God's eyes, then what is of paramount importance in the life of a man? How do we determine what is true masculinity? From God's point of view, what is the true measure of a man?

A NEW PERSPECTIVE

Many years ago, someone shared with me words from the apostle Paul in the book of Romans (8:28) where God declares that all circumstances in a person's life are working together for that person's good. That thought gave me a great deal of encouragement, particularly when I realized that life was full of difficulty. The problem for me was how to interpret the word *good*.

Sure, I wanted the "good life" and thought that was what God wanted for me. However, I had interpreted the good life to mean achievement, comfort, pleasure, and prosperity.

After it was pointed out to me, I soon realized the importance of looking at the next verse in Romans because verse 29 revealed what was actually good for my life in the sight of God. What I considered to be the good life was not at all what God had revealed it to be. In Romans 8:29 we are told that the ultimate good in life is that we be conformed to the image of His Son. It finally dawned on me that God's desire for me and for all men is to become more like Jesus. Up until that time, my whole life had been focused on what I was achieving and what I was experiencing. God, on the other hand, was more concerned with the type of man I was becoming.

The type of men we are becoming—isn't this exactly what Solzhenitsyn was suggesting in the quote we read in the last chapter? Prison had made him realize that the object of life was not prosperity and pleasure but rather the maturing of the soul.

Now I realize we live in a culture where men might not believe Christlikeness is very manly. I know for many years, it did not have much appeal for me. In my mind, it meant I had to be more religious, that I had to withdraw from the world and go into hiding. This is not what I desired for my life.

However, as I studied Jesus' life, I began to realize Jesus was not religious—at least not what we typically think of as being religious. He lived in a very religious culture, where many of the religious people found Him to be quite contemptible:

- He did not follow their traditions to the letter of the Law.
- Many of the religious leaders did not like the people He hung out with.
- He spoke harshly to the Pharisees and other men of learning and status.
- He made political matters worse as many of their followers began to follow Him and His teachings.

God is asking us to strive to be like Christ in all our thoughts, words, and deeds. Christlikeness is the objective, and I would readily share that such a life is not a life of self-righteousness or the absence of achievement and pleasure. Over the years, what I have come to recognize is that what Christ is simply instructing each of us to do is:

- To be transformed in our character
- To grow in wisdom
- To love, to have compassion, and to have quality relationships

Character, wisdom, and love make up the essence of what it means to be an authentic man. In fact, I would like to address the significance of each of these qualities and why it is so important that we possess them.

To Be Transformed in Our Character

A man's character is not static. Certain character qualities in our lives are either increasing or diminishing. Unfortunately, out in the world of business, a general erosion seems to be taking place in men's character. What we fail to realize is that when image and appearance become preeminent in our lives, the heart and the soul will be neglected. The ways of the commercial world can then easily eat away at our character if we do not stay on guard.

When we think of character, we generally think of honesty, integrity, diligence, fairness, and selflessness. But at the heart of character is the ability to restrain our desires. As a man grows in character, he builds the muscles of self-restraint.

I have found an obvious relationship between a man's character and his reputation. Our reputation is the way people see us. Every single person reading this book has a reputation. The way we see ourselves and the way others see us are not necessarily the same. What happens is that we so easily become consumed with what others think of us that we get caught up in image making, impressing others, and winning their approval.

In the process, against our own best interests, we compromise ourselves. Our reputation suffers. Many men do not realize that a good reputation is a by-product of a strong character. Furthermore, our character serves as a compass that guides us through life. Our character ultimately allows us to know who we are and what our lives are all about. Another way to look at it is to say that character is not about pleasure and achievement. In fact, when pleasure and achievement become the driving forces in a man's life, it generally leads to the unintended consequence of an erosion of character.

Author and speaker Ravi Zacharias has said:

> I remember one occasion when a businessman, looking back on his life, shared with me his memories of a life morally mangled. He said, "It started with my imagination that reinforced certain wrong desires. Then, having made repeated choices that were clearly wrong, in betrayal after betrayal I convinced myself that what I had indulged in I needed. The more I convinced myself that I needed it, I soon redefined who I was as a person. Now, as I look at what I have become, I can no longer live with myself. I hate who I am. I am emotionally running, but I do not know where to go."

This is a picture of a man who has lost his moral compass and who is, therefore, completely lost.

Again, our reputation is the way other people see us, while our character is who we really are. If the focus of our lives is on the development of our character and the maturing of our souls, then our reputation will take care of itself. Ultimately, we will be known for who we are and not for the impressions we make on others.

To Grow in Wisdom

According to the book of Proverbs in the Old Testament, wisdom is one of the greatest of all life's possessions. An important component of wisdom is to have the skill to see things as they really are and not just as they appear to be. This ability is so important because as we move through various seasons of life, we are continually developing ideas that explain how life works. These diverse sets of ideas govern our thinking, telling us what the world is like and how we should live in it. Wisdom will enable a man to distinguish between those ideas in life that are true and those that are false.

Stephen Covey contends that if men are truly going to lead healthy, vibrant lives, their ideas about life must be rooted in what is true. He shares a wonderful illustration that demonstrates the importance of this truth:

> Suppose you wanted to arrive at a specific location in central Chicago. A street map of the city would be a great help to you in reaching your destination. But suppose you were given the wrong map. Through a printing error, the map labeled "Chicago" was actually a map of Detroit. Can you imagine the frustration, the ineffectiveness of trying to reach your destination?
>
> You might work on your behavior—you could try harder, be more diligent, double your speed. But your efforts would only succeed in getting you to the wrong place faster.
>
> You might work on your attitude—you could think more positively. You still wouldn't get to the right place, but perhaps you wouldn't care. Your attitude would be so positive, you'd be happy wherever you were.
>
> The point is, you'd still be lost. The fundamental problem has nothing to do with your behavior or your attitude. It has everything to do with having a wrong map.
>
> If you have the right map of Chicago, then diligence be-

comes important, and when you encounter frustrating obstacles along the way, then attitude can make a real difference. But the first and most important requirement is the accuracy of the map.

This is what I have learned to be true in the lives of so many men. They are attempting to live their lives with maps that are totally inaccurate. They have false ideas about life, masculinity, work, success, and identity. This is why so many men feel truly lost when the economy, which they have no control over, turns their lives upside down. What they do not realize is that they interpret everything they experience through these false maps, these false ideas that they have mentally developed over the course of their lives.

Wisdom plays such a crucial role in our lives. The development of wisdom is one of the most prominent themes in the entire Bible. The ancients believed that the way humans most effectively dealt with the chief problems of life was wisdom. As we have also read, Pascal's solution for the struggles of life that come from embracing false ideas is simply to uproot them and replace them with wisdom. Now read Solomon's words in Proverbs 3:13-18 regarding the importance of wisdom:

How blessed is the man who finds wisdom,
And the man who gains understanding.
For its profit is better than the profit of silver
And its gain better than fine gold.
She is more precious than jewels;
And nothing you desire compares with her.
Long life is in her right hand;
In her left hand are riches and honor.
Her ways are pleasant ways,
And all her paths are peace.
She is a tree of life to those who take hold of her,
And happy are all who hold her fast.

As I read these words, it is hard not to conclude that, yes, wisdom is one of the most valuable possessions in life, particularly when we hone in on these particular words:

She is more precious than jewels;
And nothing you desire compares with her.

We live in a time where we are flooded with information, and many people are convinced that they have a real advantage in life if they have a great deal of knowledge. Yet every day we read of many brilliant fools who ruin their lives, their businesses, and their families by making bad decisions. Many very knowledgeable people lack wisdom.

What we fail to recognize is that the *quantity* of what we know is not of ultimate importance. What matters is the *quality* of what we know. The quality of our knowledge is at the heart of wisdom.

Author Richard Foster believes that superficiality is the curse of the modern age. He contends that the desperate need of our day is not for a greater number of intelligent or gifted people but for a greater number of wiser people who have depth to their lives. He believes wisdom is the answer to a hollow world.

Unfortunately, most modern men seem to dismiss the nature and value of wisdom to the point where it is no longer of real importance to them. I think for most of us the distractions and the frantic pace of a technological culture does not encourage deep thought, reflection, or introspection.

Furthermore, most people believe the ultimate outcome of their lives depends on the moral choices they make. If they make good moral choices, these people think their lives will go well. And certainly, bad moral choices can wreck a person's life. But this is only partially true. Wisdom deals with true clarity in our thinking, and this is why we so treasure it. It is much, much more than just being moral and good.

Wisdom is knowing what to do in all situations, not just moral situations. As a matter of fact, wisdom applies in the vast majority of life's situations in which moral rules have only nominal application. The first time I read this thought as it was developed by Tim Keller, I was so grateful for his remarkable gift of insight. He contends that most of the choices and decisions we make each day are not specifically moral choices. Seen in this context, my perspective shifted, and I now clearly understand that wisdom incorporates judgment as well as morality.

For example, the following are some of the pivotal but not essentially moral driven issues in our lives:

• Career choice/career change
• Dealing with your teenager
• Financial decisions
• Investment decisions

And there are questions we have such as:

• Should I confront someone?
• Should I take this risk?
• How should I spend my time?
• What are my priorities?

Wisdom is a combination of sound judgment and moral choice; together they complement each other, and the consequences from such combined choices will ultimately shape our lives.

Wisdom, then, offers us insight into the true nature of

things—both physical and spiritual reality. Wisdom allows us to grow in competence as we respond to the realities of life. Wisdom is knowing how things really work and why things happen, and then knowing what to do about it.

Wisdom is knowing how things really work
and knowing why things happen, and then knowing
what to do about it.

The Bible says that God designed life according to wisdom; therefore, there is a pattern or fabric to all of reality. It is the wisdom we acquire that enables us to perceive that pattern or fabric and live in harmony with it.

LOVE, COMPASSION, AND QUALITY RELATIONSHIPS

Joe Ehrmann says the true mark of a man is found in the quality of his relationships—the capacity you have to love and be loved. When you look over your life at the end of it, the only thing that is really going to matter is the relationships you have had.

There are so many important relationships in life. We could talk about marriage or our relationships with our children, but here are a couple of observations about friendships with other men. I believe this is such an important issue because friendships and quality relationships among men are hard to come by, yet friendship can bring something into our lives that marriage and family cannot.

Dr. Eugene Kennedy, a psychology professor at Loyola University, in an interview with *U.S. News and World Report*, had some interesting thoughts on friendship that were primarily directed toward men:

> There is a profound longing for friendship, a poignant searching for the kinds of things that only close and lasting relationships give you. But people have difficulty in knowing how to go about making friends because our society has told them self-gratification will make them successful and happy. Therefore people are not on good enough terms with themselves and don't appreciate the simple things about their own character. They think they have to be something other than what they are.

Again, I return to the book *Season of Life*. In Jeffrey Marx's interview with him, Coach Joe Ehrmann laments the fact that men are always comparing and competing, wondering how they measure up to other men. It leaves them with feelings of isolation and loneliness. Coach Ehrmann mentions a study he had read that revealed a sad fact: most men over the age of thirty-five have no authentic friends—someone close to them whom they can be vulnerable with and share their innermost thoughts and feelings.

Armond Nicholi Jr., in his book *The Question of God*, tells about C. S. Lewis' view of friendship. Lewis, for years an atheist, had a very pessimistic view of life and had no friends. As a Christian, his view of life and relationships was transformed. As Nicholi put it, nothing brought Lewis more enjoyment than sitting around a fire with a group of close friends engaged in good discussion, or taking long walks with them through the English countryside:

> "My happiest hours," Lewis wrote, "are spent with three or four old friends in old clothes tramping together and putting up in small pubs—or else sitting up till the small hours in someone's college rooms, talking nonsense, poetry, theology, metaphysics .. . There's no sound I like better than . . . laughter." In another

letter to his friend Greeves, Lewis writes: "friendship is the greatest of worldly goods. Certainly, to me it is the chief happiness of life. If I had to give a piece of advice to a young man about a place to live, I think I shd. [sic] say, 'sacrifice almost everything you have to live where you can be near your friends.' Lewis changed from a wary introvert with very few close relationships to a personable extrovert with scores of close friends and colleagues. George Sayer, a biographer who knew Lewis for some thirty years, and Owen Barfield, a close friend for over forty years, described Lewis after his [conversion] "He was unusually cheerful, and took an almost boyish delight" in life. [They] describe him as "great fun, an extremely witty and amusing companion . . . considerate . . . more concerned with the welfare of his friends than with himself."

I think Lewis recognized that without great friendships, life is virtually bankrupt. Furthermore, it strikes me that really good friendships have to be deliberately pursued and forged over time. And when we are willing to come out of hiding, be vulnerable, and be willing to share our secrets with a close friend or two, these friendships will deepen. It seems that the power to honor the truth and speak the truth openly are at the heart of being a healthy, authentic man.

So when we think of manhood and masculinity, we should recognize that character, wisdom, and our ability to love others are at the heart of being a man. As we consider these components of true manhood, we need to ask the question, *How can I make them become realities in my life?*

The answer is: we can't; at least not on our own strength and power. The truth is we do not have the resources within ourselves to produce these qualities. Augustine realized how feeble and weak we are and therefore understood he needed something outside of himself to come and transform his life—something or someone who could come and enable him to do that which he could not do in his own strength. He realized that person could only be God. Only God can bring forth the transformation we need by strengthening our hearts, enlightening our minds, and giving us a greater capacity to love.

A FOOL'S ERRAND PAID IN FOOL'S GOLD

There is a parable in the book of Luke (12:15-21) that has a great deal of relevance to people in the world of business. John Ortberg has taken this parable and retells it in a modern setting. Though he lengthens the story a good bit, he drives home the core truth that Jesus was teaching in the parable.

> There was a very successful man who owned a very successful business. Like many successful people, he was consumed with his work. He did what it took to get the job done. Even when he wasn't working, his mind would always drift back to the business.
>
> At home his wife was continually trying to get him to slow down, to spend more time at home. He was vaguely aware that the kids were growing up and he was missing it. However, the kids had come to the point of not expecting much from him.
>
> He would continually think to himself, "I will be more available next year when things settle down. He however, never seems to notice that things do not ever settle down.
>
> He continually reminds himself and his wife, "I am doing it for you and the kids."
>
> His wife [urges] him [to go] to church and he goes on occasion, but he prefers to sleep in because it is the only day to do so. He would have more time for church when things settled down.
>
> One night, he felt a twinge of pain in his chest and his wife rushes him to the hospital. He has suffered a mild heart attack. His doctor informs him of the changes he must make in his lifestyle. So he cuts down on red meat and ice cream, and begins an exercise program. Soon, he feels much better and all the pain goes away. Eventually he lets things slide, reminding himself

that he will get in better shape when things settle down.

One day, the CFO of his company comes in to see him. He is told by the CFO that their business is booming to the point that "we cannot keep up with all the orders. We have the chance to strike the 'mother lode.' If we can catch this wave we can all be set for life. However, we need larger facilities, new equipment, and the new state of the art technology and delivery systems to keep up with all our orders."

So the man becomes more consumed with his work, every waking moment is devoted to this once in a lifetime opportunity.

He tells his wife, "You know what this means don't you? When I am through with this new phase, I will be able to relax. We will be set for life. I have covered all the bases, prepared for every contingency. We will be financially secure and can finally take all those trips you have been wanting to go on." She, of course, had heard this before, so she did not get her hopes up too much.

At about 11 o'clock that night, she tells her husband she is going up to bed and asked him if he was ready to go up with her. "You go ahead. I will be up in a minute, I have one thing I want to finish . . ." as he sat in front of his computer.

She goes up, falls asleep, and wakes up at 3 in the morning. She realizes her husband is not in bed. She goes down stairs to get him and finds him asleep in front of the computer. She reaches out to wake him up, but his skin is cold. He does not respond. She gets this sick feeling in the pit of her stomach and dials 911.

By the time the paramedics arrive they tell her he died of a massive heart attack some hours ago.

His death is the major item of discussion in the financial community. His extensive obituary was written up in all the papers. It is a shame he was dead, for he would have loved to have read all the good things written about him.

They have a memorial service and because of his prominence, the whole community comes out for it. Several people get up to eulogize him at the service. One said, "He was one of the leading entrepreneurs of the day; he was a real leader." Another said, "He was a real innovator in new technology and delivery systems." A third said, "He was a man of principles, would never cheat anyone." It was noted by many that he was a pillar in the community and was known and liked by everyone. His life was truly a success.

Then they buried him and they all went home. Late that night, in the cemetery, an angel of God comes along and makes his way through all of the markers and tombstones. He stands before this man's memorial tombstone and tracks with his finer the single word God has chosen to summarize this man's life. If you are familiar with the parable you know the word. "Fool."

Listen to Jesus' simple and direct conclusion to the parable in Luke 12:20-21:

> *"You fool! This very night your soul is required of you; and now who will own what you have prepared? So is the man who lays up treasure for himself, and is not rich toward God"* [and the things of God].

This makes me realize that my greatest fear should never be fear of failure, but the fear of actually investing my entire life in something that does not really matter. Jesus is revealing that this is what this man has done.

In *Season of Life*, Ehrmann says that true masculinity involves investing your life in a cause that is bigger than your own individual hopes, dreams, and desires. We live in a culture that measures greatness by building a business, amassing some large fortune, or being a celebrity. But in my mind true greatness is measured by the impact you make on the lives of other people. But the man in the parable had no interest in that. Now I don't know about you, but what I find most compelling in this parable is when Jesus says, "So is the man who lays up treasure for himself, and is not rich toward God."

What is Jesus saying when He refers to being rich toward God or finding the true riches of life? What in this life has God identified as having such true value? In one sense, I think we have already identified them:

- *A man's character:* A good name is more desirable than great wealth (Proverbs 22:1).
- *The gaining of wisdom:* More valuable than silver and gold; nothing you desire compares with it (Proverbs 3:13-18).
- *The quality of our relationships:* Nothing is of greater value than our relationships; they are truly priceless (1 John 4:7).

And finally, the apostle Paul, a wealthy Pharisee, had to sacrifice all of his wealth and power when he became a Christian. However, he gladly parted with all of his worldly trappings because he found the most valuable possession in all of life:

I consider everything worthless in comparison to the unsurpassing value of knowing Christ Jesus my Lord for whom I suffered the loss of all things, and consider it rubbish, so that I might gain this relationship with Christ (Philippians 3:8, author paraphrase).

Paul said this relationship had changed all his worldly ambitions in life. Christianity is not about following a bunch of rules and religious practices. It is about knowing Christ personally and walking through life with Him.

As I get older, the sad truth I find in so many men's lives is that they do not want God. They may believe in Him, they may seek His favor by going to church, they certainly want Him to bless them, but they do not want to know Him, be close to Him, or allow Him to guide them through life.

⚒

[Men] do not want God. They may believe in Him,
they may seek His favor by going to church, they
certainly want Him to bless them, but they do not
want to know Him and be close to Him . . .

⚒

I have a friend, a local physician, who will tell you that his life
was radically turned around spiritually when he heard these words
spoken of Jesus from the Sermon on the Mount, Matthew 7:21-23:

> *Not everyone who calls me, "Lord, Lord," will enter into the kingdom
> of heaven . . . Many will say to me on the judgment day: "Lord, Lord,
> did we not preach in your name, and cast out demons in your name,
> and do many great works in your name? . . . Then I shall tell them
> plainly, I never knew you, depart from me . . .* (author paraphrase).

My friend said that when he heard those words, "I never knew
you," he recognized Christ was talking about him. He was, he ac-
knowledged, "a good church-going man who believed in Jesus but
did not know Him." This is why Paul tells us that nothing in life
can be compared to the incredible value of knowing Christ. For not
only does this relationship have the power to transform our lives, it
is also the true mark of a person who God welcomes into His
kingdom.

PROFOUND YET SO VERY SIMPLE

I was very moved by the words of Dr. Peter Moore, as he reflected on his twenty-fifth reunion at Yale:

> Returning to my twenty-fifth reunion at Yale, I watched as
> Mercedes-Benz's disgorged prosperous-looking members of the

Class of 1958 and their wives at the gates of the Old Campus. The program announced that former classmates were preparing to tell the rest of us about the lessons they had learned climbing ladders to success. Wandering along familiar campus pathways that first evening of the reunion, two questions weighed heavily on my mind: "Had I been a success? . . . What was success?" The occasion, redolent with nostalgia, demanded such questions be asked and answers at least attempted. After all, what had one to show for all that expensive education after a quarter of a century?

I tried to be as honest with myself as I could be. I refused to take easy refuge in pat answers that, after all, I had started this and done that. While I was thus musing suddenly I remembered that a friend who was rector of a nearby church had invited me to join him and a handful of parishioners for their customary 5:00 P.M. Evening Prayer. I hurried across campus to St. John's and took my place as the service opened, still very troubled by the questions I couldn't shake from my mind.

We came in time to a familiar part of the service, recorded in Luke 2, where the aged Simeon picks up the Christ child in the Temple and blesses God with the words: "Lord, now lettest thou thy servant depart in peace, according to thy word; for mine eyes have seen thy salvation." Listening to these words, I felt a quiet assurance settle in my soul. All the anticipation of wise old Simeon's many years found joyous fulfillment in one moment's realization that there in his arms was the long-awaited Messiah. Such was the sense of completeness that his knowledge gave him, he was now ready to "depart—or die—in peace."

In the quiet of that service I discovered what real success was. It came to me quietly, but very clearly, that the only thing worth calling success was coming to the knowledge of God and being able to behold him in the face of his Son. It seemed to me a knowledge so profound and yet so simple that it made even the smallest accomplishment of great importance when done in its light.

These words of Dr. Moore, found in his book *Disarming the Secular Gods*, remind me of David's final words of wisdom to his son Solomon, uttered just as he was about to die:

As for you, my son Solomon, know the God of your father, and serve Him with a whole heart and a willing mind; for the Lord searches all hearts, and understands every intent of the thoughts. If you seek Him, He will let you find Him; but if you forsake Him, He will reject you forever (1 Chronicles 28:9).

Notice, King David does not say be a good king, lead a good life, believe in God. No, to the contrary, he says it is crucial that you know God. He is telling Solomon that if he gets this right the rest of his life will fall into place. And perhaps most important to men struggling in today's world are King David's words:

If you seek Him, He will let you find Him.

If this is true, then every single one of us—today, right now, in this very moment—is as close to God as we want to be—as we choose to be.

PART III · A LIFE WELL LIVED

Where is the Life we have lost in living?

Where is the wisdom we have lost in knowledge?

Where is the knowledge we have lost in information?

—*T. S. Eliot, Choruses from "The Rock"*

6

LIFE'S GREATEST PARADOX

The long painful history of the world is for
people to be tempted to choose prestige and
power over love, being in charge over being
led, being served over serving others.

—*Henri Nouwen*

A number of years ago, I met several times with a man whom I would describe as an agnostic. He was a bright, well-educated individual, who clearly was searching for spiritual truth. After about six months, he came by my office and announced that he was ready to become a Christian. I was so surprised you could almost have picked me up off the floor.

One of the primary reasons, he told me, that he had come to this decision was because, in his search, so much of what he had read in the Bible was counterintuitive. Scriptural teachings went against the grain of natural human instinct and reason. He said he had concluded that the Bible, and the wisdom of the Bible, could not have been inspired by mere man.

So many of God's important truths are foreign to the world we live in because they are in fact counterintuitive. Up seems to be down; down seems to be up. For this reason, biblical truth comes off as utter foolishness to some people.

What these people do not recognize is that very often the wisdom of God, the truth of God, is paradoxical. Paradox is defined in Webster's as: "a tenet that is contrary to received opinion. A statement or principle that is seemingly contradictory and opposed to common sense, but may in fact be true."

NOT YOUR AVERAGE PARADOX

I want to lay out for you a paradox that is essential to a life well lived. However, what I would like to share with you is not merely an average paradox; it is what I like to call "Life's Greatest Paradox." This paradox strikes right at the heart of us as men, and its ramifications are incredibly significant in all areas of our lives— in our work lives, in our relational lives, and in our spiritual lives. It is of foundational importance if you want to live an exceptional life.

Simply stated, life's greatest paradox can be summed up in the words, *True strength is found in humility*. The apostle Paul tells us as much in 2 Corinthians 12 when he reveals a struggle in his own life with what he calls "a thorn in the flesh." He asks God to remove the pain and the suffering of this affliction. God's response is no, and instead He tells Paul: "My grace is sufficient for you, for power is perfected in weakness."

I don't know about you, but to my mind, this is a very interesting and challenging concept. It's certainly not taught at Harvard

Business School, and it is clearly counterintuitive. Paul is revealing that inner strength is found only when we are willing to acknowledge our weaknesses, our deficiencies, and our inadequacies as we humble ourselves. Paul reinforces the paradox when he said, "When I am weak, then I am strong."

I like to think of this more as a mystery than a principle because it can only be true with God's grace, without which it would be utter foolishness. Only with God's grace can we find true strength, and it comes from acknowledging our weaknesses as we humble ourselves before Him. It is a strength that carries us through the toughest of times. It is the strength that provides us the power to change our lives.

As we explore the underpinnings to this paradox, we would best be served by first taking a careful look at the biblical concept of weakness. Let's approach the problem indirectly by first considering the thorny issue of pride.

PRIDE AND ARROGANCE

If the paradox of finding strength in humility is true, then we can logically conclude that pride and arrogance are what make men weak.

I find myself often being questioned by men about the semantics of the word *pride* more than almost any other word in the Bible. When I use it, I am not talking about taking pride in your work, your family, or your achievements as it bears on your individual gifts and your striving for excellence.

When the Bible speaks of pride, it refers to arrogance, "a feeling of superiority." The Greek word for pride is *hubris*, "taking too high a view of oneself." And not coincidentally it is in the loftiness of hubris where we find an overarching ambition that has felled many a heroic figure in the dramatic arts.

As you read these words, you might be thinking, *I don't have a problem with pride. It is not something I struggle with. Now, Joe, my neighbor; and Tom, my business associate; and Bill, from college—yes, but not me!*

You may be familiar with these words of C. S. Lewis from his classic book *Mere Christianity*:

> There is one vice of which no man in the world is free; which everyone in the world loathes when he sees it in someone else; and of which hardly any people, except Christians, ever imagine that they are guilty themselves . . . I do not think I have ever heard anyone who was not a Christian accuse himself of this vice . . . There is no fault which makes a man more unpopular, and no fault which we are more unconscious of in ourselves. And the more we have it ourselves, the more we dislike it in others.

What an incredibly powerful line that C. S. Lewis has written: "And the more we have it [pride and arrogance] ourselves, the more we dislike it in others." Is this a paradox within a paradox?

Lewis, however, saves his most powerful words for his concluding point:

> The vice I am speaking of is Pride or Self-Conceit . . . Pride leads to every other vice: it is the complete anti-God state of mind.

Lewis is telling us that pride and arrogance—the anti-God state of mind—is so deadly because it is so insidious. It slowly grows and develops in our lives, becoming well-established without our knowledge. Furthermore, it is aggressive in nature, and it creates in us a desire to be superior—I am content with my wealth only when I'm wealthier than you, for example.

Doesn't this help us to understand why we are always comparing ourselves to others? Think about how we secretly compare ourselves, our accomplishments, our lifestyles, and even our kids to other people's kids. We envy; we compare; we are all at risk of being arrogant.

I believe at times we all find ourselves subject to the pull of comparison, the yearning for admiration and fame. After all, these are the measurements of worldly success. Arrogance and pride, however, unlike true and humble contentment for a job well done in the service of others, lead us down a slippery and destructive path as we try to impress others. They often cause us to inflate and embellish our successes and accomplishments in the process.

But I would like to point out that there is an even darker side to pride. Our pride as men explains why we fear the threat of shame and why we are always trying to hide our weaknesses, our failures, our fears, our addictions, and our struggles with depression. In essence, pride is what leads us to hide who we really are.

Philosopher Blaise Pascal, in his famous work the *Pensées*, explains the corrosive power of pride and how it leads men to conceal themselves from others:

> It is the nature of self-esteem and of the human self to love only oneself and to consider oneself alone. But what can a man do? He wants to be great and finds that he is small; he wants to be happy and finds that he is unhappy; he wants to be perfect and finds that he is riddled with imperfections; he wants to be the object of men's affection and esteem and sees that his faults deserve only their dislike and contempt. The embarrassing position in which he finds himself produces in him the most unjust and criminal passion that can possibly be imagined; he conceives a mortal hatred of the truth which brings him down to earth and convinces him of his faults. He would like to be able to annihilate it, and, not being able to destroy it in himself, he destroys it in the minds of other people. That is to say, he concentrates all his efforts on concealing his faults both from others and from

himself, and cannot stand being made to see them or their being seen by other people.

Have you ever thought about how much different your life would be if you did not fear and worry about what others thought of you, if you never had to impress anyone? If what Pascal says is true, it makes me wonder if we ever really know who we are.

If we cannot be transparent with ourselves and also cannot be transparent with others, then who are we? Tim Keller amplifies Blaise Pascal's thinking, saying:

> All of us, without God's help, live lives of illusion. We spend almost all of our lives trying to prove to other people and ourselves that we are something other than what we really are.

Several years ago, an article appeared in the *Harvard Business Review* on why leaders in various business organizations fail. The core data came from a study that revealed the four primary factors that brought about the failures of those senior leaders:

- They were *authoritarian*—controlling, demanding, not listening to others.
- They were *autonomous*—little accountability, aloof, and isolated.
- They committed *adultery*.
- They became more and more *arrogant*.

I believe the underlying reason these leaders encountered failure could be summed up by these words from the study: feeling and acting as if they were superior to all others. If you think you are superior to all others in your organization, you will find yourself believing that you can treat people however you want, sleep with whomever you choose, and spend the organization's money at will. Basically, you believe you can do whatever you want. When Senator John Edwards confessed to having sexual relations with a woman in his campaign, his explanation was, in essence, that he had arrived at a point where he did not think the rules applied to him.

Martin Luther, a true man of God, at a certain point in his life recognized that his giving to the poor was for all the wrong reasons:

> I realized I don't help the poor to help the poor; I do it so I can feel noble. So, I can be recognized. I do it for me, out of pride and self-centeredness.

Have you ever thought about why you do the good things you do? Could it be that it is because, as the prominent British journalist Malcolm Muggeridge once said, "Men are trapped in the deep dark dungeon of their egos"?

Humility helps you to recognize that all you are
and all you have is a gift from God and a result of
other people contributing to your life.

A HEART OF GRATITUDE

Humility, on the other hand, allows us to truly understand our place in the universe, to understand God's place for us, and to see ourselves as God sees us. You have infinite and inherent value, but you are of no greater value than anyone else.

In the Old Testament, Moses said that arrogance is looking at your life, your abilities, and your achievements, and thinking in your heart that it is your strength, your power, and your ability that has led to all of your success. Humility helps you to recognize that all you are and all you have is a gift from God and a result of other people contributing to your life. Read the following example from Drayton Nabers Jr.'s book *The Case for Character*:

> Let's take the example of a tailback who wins the Heisman Trophy. This Heisman winner gets his name in the paper and his face on ESPN. But where did he get the DNA that created the strong body? And where did he get the great coordination that helped him win the prize? How many of the one hundred trillion cells in his body did he create?
>
> We are told that for each of these cells there is a bank of instructions more detailed than the thirty-two volumes of the *Encyclopedia Britannica* put together. Does this tailback understand even one of these instructions? (For that matter, does even the smartest doctor or biologist in the world fully understand the marvel of a single human cell?)
>
> "But I worked so hard," the tailback might say. "I went to the weight room. I practiced harder than anyone else on the team."
>
> To him we could reply: "But who taught you to work that hard? Who built the weight room? Who bought the equipment? Who built the university, including the stadium you played in? Who cut the grass there and laid out the lines and boundaries? Did you hire or pay your coaches? Did you recruit your teammates? Did you open up those holes in the line that you ran through?"
>
> If this tailback has humility, he will express nothing but overflowing gratitude when he wins the Heisman—to his parents, to his teachers, to his coaches, to all the players on his team, to everyone who helped him along the way. Most of all, time and time again, he will express gratitude to God.

In describing humility, Nabers states:

. . . humility is a form of wisdom. It is thinking clearly. It is simply being realistic. It is knowing who really deserves the credit and the glory for what we do.

There is a wonderful true story along these same lines in Stephen K. Scott's inspiration, *The Richest Man Who Ever Lived*:

> My former church pastor, Dr. Jim Borror, while visiting a church in the Northwest, was asked by a woman to meet with her husband, a multimillionaire entrepreneur with thousands of employees. Although this man had tens of millions of dollars and everything money could buy, he was unhappy, bitter, and cantankerous. No one liked being around him, and contention and strife followed him wherever he went. He was disliked by his employees and even his children. His wife barely tolerated him.
>
> When he met the man, Dr. Borror listened to him talk about his accomplishments and quickly realized that pride ruled this man's heart and mind. He claimed he had single-handedly built his company from scratch. Even his parents hadn't given him a dime. He had worked his way through college.
>
> Jim said, "So you did everything by yourself."
>
> "Yep," the man replied.
>
> Jim repeated, "No one ever gave you anything."
>
> "Nothing!"
>
> So Jim asked, "Who changed your diapers? Who fed you as a baby? Who taught you how to read and write? Who gave you jobs that enabled you to work your way through college? Who gave you your first job after college? Who serves food in your company's cafeteria? Who cleans the toilets in your company's rest rooms?" The man hung his head in shame. Moments later, with tears in his eyes, he said, "Now that I think about it, I haven't accomplished anything by myself. Without the kindness and efforts of others, I probably wouldn't have anything." Jim nodded and asked, "Don't you think they deserve a little thanks?"
>
> That man's heart was transformed, seemingly overnight. In the months that followed, he wrote thank-you letters to every person he could think of who had made a contribution to his

life. He wrote thank-you notes to every one of his 3,000 employees. He not only felt a deep sense of gratitude, he began to treat everyone around him with respect and appreciation.

When Dr. Borror visited him a year or two later, he could hardly recognize him. Happiness and peace had replaced the anger and contention in his heart. He looked years younger. His employees loved him for treating them with the honor and respect that true humility engenders.

It should strike us all after reading this that humble people are grateful people. They give thanks to those who really deserve the credit. Thanksgiving in one sense is a way we humble ourselves. It is a way to acknowledge that all we are and all we have is a gift from God. This is why Dr. Hans Selye, who was the true pioneer in discovering the impact of emotions on health, at the end of his life concluded from all his years of research, that a heart of gratitude is the single most nourishing attitude for a person's good health and well-being.

WHAT DOES HUMILITY LOOK LIKE?

I have found that most people do not really know what humility looks like. Historically, humility has been linked to the word *meekness*. In the beatitudes we hear the words, "Blessed are the meek, for they shall inherit the earth." Of course, meekness rhymes with weakness, so who in the world could possibly want to be meek? I have never heard a father say, "I want my son to grow up and be meek."

The word meekness surprisingly comes from the word *praus*, a powerful animal that knows how to restrain its power. The idea here is that meek and humble people are powerful people, though they do not flaunt their strength and power.

The Bible teaches in both the Old and New Testaments that

God desires to give His strength and power to His people. It is God's gift of fortitude, an inner strength, which will enable us to be the men we are meant to be, the men we want to be. Various words are used to describe this—His strength, His power, His might. There is a unique word that is very often used in Scripture to describe the power God imparts to us—the word "grace."

Grace is God's life in us, where God enables us to do that which we cannot do by ourselves. It is divine enablement. We see its significance in salvation and in our day-to-day living. God makes it very clear: He gives His grace only to humble people (James 4:6, 1 Peter 5:5).

A number of years ago, Jim Collins, who was a faculty member at the Stanford University Graduate School of Business, wrote a best-selling book titled *Built to Last*. It was based on a management study of companies he and his associates performed back in the 1990s with the intent of analyzing and demonstrating how great companies sustain themselves over time.

In studying the data, Collins came up with the idea of trying to determine if certain universal characteristics distinguished truly great companies. Using tough benchmarks, Collins and his research team identified eleven elite companies that were doing a good job and which, for some reason, produced phenomenal results for fifteen consecutive years (some of these companies included Abbott Labs, Kimberly Clark, and Nucor Steel). He and his team then sought to determine how these companies made the leap from being *good* companies to being *great* companies. He took the results of all this intensive research and wrote what would come to be one of the best- selling business books ever published, *Good to Great*.

What I find interesting is that Collins said he gave his research team explicit instructions to downplay the role of top executives. He did not believe that the business community needed another book on leadership. Although he had insisted they ignore the role of the company executives, the research team kept pushing back. They soon came to recognize something very unusual about the executives in these good-to-great companies.

They went back and forth until, as Collins put it, "the data won." They recognized that all the executives from these good-to-great companies were cut from the same cloth. They all were what he called "Level 5 Leaders."

Collins wrote, "Level 5 Leaders are a study in duality: modest and willful, humble and fearless." These good-to-great leaders never desired to be celebrities or to be lifted up on a pedestal. Collins declared that they were "seemingly ordinary people quietly producing extraordinary results." What Collins and his team of researchers clearly observed is that a Level 5 Leader builds enduring greatness through the paradoxical blend of personal humility and professional will. In essence, a Level 5 Leader lives out Life's Greatest Paradox.

Tim Keller makes a similar observation when he says, "The humble are kind and gentle, but also brave and fearless. If you are to be humble, you cannot have one without the other."

This is where Life's Greatest Paradox moves beyond concept into reality, particularly when one begins to live the humble life and begins to experience the extraordinary power God's grace unleashes in your life. Strength, indeed, is found in humility, and that strength, as Paul so well understood, is a gift of God.

BOTH LION AND LAMB

We find a number of biblical examples of this level of leadership in men like John the Baptist, the apostle Paul, and Moses. In one of my favorite examples of true humility in a man, in Numbers 12:3, we learn that Moses was the most humble man on the face of the earth. Yet we see Moses go before the most powerful man on earth at the time—Pharaoh, king of Egypt—who could have easily had him killed if he so desired. Moses stood before Pharaoh and said to him, with great boldness, "I want you to let my people go—I want you to give up your entire slave labor force, the key to your entire economic and military superiority. I want you to do it without payment. And I don't want you to mess around; I want you do it quickly" (author's paraphrase of the story found in Exodus 5-12).

This polarity of characteristics you find in the truly humble—kind but fearless, gentle yet bold—is most clearly seen in the life of Jesus. In Revelations 5:5-6, Jesus is referred to as both a lion and a lamb. In Matthew 11, He refers to Himself as gentle and meek. He is, after all, the God of the universe who has restrained His power to become one of us.

First, read the words of Napoleon at the end of his life:

> I die before my time and my body shall be given back to the earth and devoured by worms. What an abysmal gulf between my deep miseries and the eternal Kingdom of Christ. I marvel that whereas the ambitious dreams of myself and of Alexander and of Caesar should have vanished into thin air, a Judean peasant—Jesus—should be able to stretch his hands across the centuries and control the destinies of men and nations.

Here are three famous men—Alexander the Great, Caesar, and Napoleon—seeking to control the world by power. When we see their lives contrasted with one man, Jesus, the humble life of a carpenter, we marvel at how truly extraordinary He must have been such that the world could have been so powerfully changed through his simple life of humility.

Now read the words of James Stewart, a Scottish philosopher and minister:

When I speak of the mystery of personality in Christ, I am

thinking of the startling coalescence of contrariety that you find in Jesus. He was the meekest and lowliest of all the sons of men, yet He said that he would come on the clouds of heaven in the glory of God. He was so austere that evil spirits and demons cried out in terror at his coming, yet he was so genial, winsome, and approachable that children loved to play with Him, and the little ones nestled in His arms. No one was ever half so kind or compassionate towards sinners, yet no one ever spoke such red hot scorching words about sin. He would not break the bruised reed and His whole life was love, yet on one occasion He demanded of the Pharisees how they expected to escape the damnation of hell. He was a dreamer of dreams and a seer of visions yet for sheer stark naked realism He has all of our self-styled realists beaten. He was a servant of all, washing the disciples' feet, yet masterfully he strode into the Temple, and the hucksters and traders fell over one another in their mad rush to get away from the fire they saw blazing in His eyes. There is nothing in History to compare with the life of Christ.

The biblical understanding is that the humble are the strongest. They don't make decisions by sticking their fingers in the air to see what other people think. They enjoy fortitude, an inner strength that comes only through God's grace. They know who they are. Their lives are not consumed by trying to please and impress others.

The humble are the strongest. They don't make
decisions by sticking their fingers in the air . . .
They know who they are. Their lives are not
consumed by trying to please
and impress others.

Conversely, the prideful feel as though they are superior to others and have this need to impress them. Although they believe themselves to be great and powerful, in reality they are crippled with a sense of inferiority and insecurity. They are extremely needy. They need to feed their egos; they need compliments; they need to be stroked; they need to be recognized. Though they do not realize it, the proud are clearly quite weak.

AN OPINION THAT COUNTS

I think we all recognize that who we are as men and what we do with our lives are greatly influenced by the opinions of others. Without realizing it, we gear our lives to meet the expectations of other people. It is sometimes hard for me to believe that I will allow other people's opinions to determine the way I see myself and how I am going to live my life. This seems, however, to be the natural tendency of all human beings. Even the ancient prophet Isaiah asked this very penetrating question:

> *Why do you have such a high regard for man—Whose breath is in his nostrils, Why do we esteem him so highly?* (Isaiah 2:22, author paraphrase)

Isaiah wanted to know why we value man and his opinions. Why do we allow their opinions of us to be such a powerful force in our lives?

George Will shares an amusing story in his popular book about baseball *Men at Work*:

> Baseball umpires are carved from granite . . . They are professional dispensers of pure justice. Once when Babe Pinelli called Babe Ruth out on strikes, Ruth made a populist argument. Ruth reasoned fallaciously (as populists do) from raw numbers to

moral weight: "There's 40,000 people here who know that last one was a ball, tomato head."

Pinelli replied with the measured stateliness of John Marshall: "Maybe so, but mine is the only opinion that counts."

When it gets right down to it, whose opinion of my life counts most? When you get to the end of your life, whose opinion will matter the most? Isaiah finds it quite incredible that mankind's opinion is far more important to us than the holy and infinite God.

Humility comes powerfully into our lives when God becomes the audience we perform for. When this happens, human opinion becomes less and less important to us.

THE CONTRITE TAX COLLECTOR

Men are not only prideful when it comes to wealth, achievement, physical appearance, and knowledge, but we also seem to naturally suffer from spiritual pride. The influential philosopher Soren Kierkegaard said that spiritual pride leads us to believe we can run our lives, achieve prosperity, and find a purpose big enough to give meaning in life—and we can do it all without God. We really don't need Him.

Spiritual pride deceives us into believing that we are good people who are in good standing with God. We come to believe that only good people get into God's kingdom; the bad people, thankfully, are kept out. But this is clearly not the teaching of Christianity. In reality, it is the humble who are let in, and it is the proud and self-righteous who are out.

Humility is the lens through which we are able to see God; and as we come to know Him, it enables us to see ourselves as we really are. This is what Jesus was communicating in His parable of the Pharisee and the tax collector:

"Two men went up into the temple to pray, one a Pharisee and the other a tax collector.

"The Pharisee stood and was praying this to himself: 'God, I thank You that I am not like other people: swindlers, unjust, adulterers, or even like this tax collector. I fast twice a week; I pay tithes of all that I get.'

"But the tax collector, standing some distance away, was even unwilling to lift up his eyes to heaven, but was beating his breast, saying, 'God, be merciful to me, the sinner!'

"I tell you, this man went to his house justified rather than the other; for everyone who exalts himself will be humbled, but he who humbles himself will be exalted" (Luke 18:9-14, author paraphrase).

One of the first things in this parable that stands out is how the proud Pharisee compares himself to the tax collector when he says, "I thank You I am not like other people . . . even like this tax collector." This Pharisee clearly displays an attitude of moral and spiritual superiority. The tax gatherer, on the other hand, sees only his sin and his need for forgiveness. He is truly humbled by virtue of recognizing his need for forgiveness of his sin.

George Carey, the former Archbishop of Canterbury, made an observation about this parable that provides great insight. This very religious, moral Pharisee, who believed in God, felt very good about himself. He was comfortable with his standing with God. Yet his pride blinded him, and he did not realize that something was terribly wrong with his life and he was not justified before God. He was not forgiven of his sin, yet the humble tax gatherer—all the while bowing in his humility and contriteness—was justified before God and forgiven of his sin. At that moment you see a picture of a spiritually healthy and vibrant man—a man who was in right relationship with God.

KNOW GOD, KNOW YOURSELF, KNOW THE DIFFERENCE

So what do we do about this deadly pride with which we are all afflicted? C. S. Lewis has written that if we are to acquire humility, we need to begin by acknowledging the fact that we struggle with pride. We must admit that it is a serious issue in our lives. Lewis wrote: "[Nothing] whatever can be done before it. If you think you are not conceited, it means you are very conceited indeed."

I think we must follow the example of the tax collector, who recognized his sinfulness and confessed it before God. The heart of Christianity is the forgiveness of sins. The Christian life begins in our recognizing we are sinful people and that we need God's forgiveness. As this tax collector went before God and humbly confessed his sin, notice the response of Jesus: "This man went to his house justified."

Finally, we will have to decide who is going to be the God of our lives. Who is going to be the audience we seek to please and impress, the audience that will ultimately determine our identity.

Bob Buford, a very prosperous businessman and founder of Halftime Ministries, shares the conversation that changed his life:

> A turning point in my own life was a conversation I had twenty years ago with Michael Kami, one of this country's top strategic planners . . . I made an appointment with Mike to explore my own [future] plans. I wanted to get his professional advice about some of the options I was examining. During the course of the conversation, Mike asked me to describe my basic interests and motivations, so I began telling him about all the things that interested me. But suddenly Mike stopped me in midsentence and asked a question that changed my life—"What's in the box?"
>
> The question took me by surprise. I didn't get it at first. In the box? What does that mean? So I asked, "What do you mean by that, Mike?"

"What's central to your life at this point?" Mike said. "If there were only room for one thing in your life, what would it be?" He took a pencil and sketched out a small square on a sheet of paper and said, "From what you're telling me, Bob, there are two things at the top of your list of priorities, your religious faith and your career." Mike indicated that the shorthand for that was a dollar sign and a cross. And he pointed at the box and said, "Before I can help you decide how to focus your interests, you have to decide: What's in the box?"

Would it be the dollar sign or the cross? Suddenly I knew I had a choice to make.

Now and then, in the midst of life's complexities, we come to a point where the options are limited and clear. This was one of those moments. What would it be for me—more money, more success, or more energy transferred to the calling I sensed so strongly? I considered those two options for a minute or so—which seemed like an eternity—and then I said, "Well, if you put it that way, it's the cross." And then I reached over to pencil a cross into Mike's box.

That one decision helped to frame everything I've done since that day. It wasn't that the small cross indicated that the work I felt called to do, to serve God, was my only loyalty in [life]. There were also family, customers, employees, recreation, and the like, but that little cross has designated the primary loyalty for my life between then and now.

This is, I believe, one of the most crucial issues in all of life. What is in your box? What is the primary loyalty in your life? For each of us, something is in the box, but are we willing to confess that it might be something other than God?

Humility is a very natural consequence when Jesus is the primary loyalty in our lives. For when Jesus is in the box, He becomes the number one audience for whom we perform. Human opinion becomes less and less important as we seek to please Him above all others. But ironically, our pride often keeps us from giving Christ the primary loyalty in our lives. In the end, many of us resist God, deliberately choosing to follow our will and our own plans.

Towards the end of his life, C. S. Lewis reached a simple conclusion about the nature of man. In the end, he concluded, there are really only two kinds of people. There are those who surrender themselves to Christ and say: "I want *Your* will to be done in my life." Then there are those who choose to go their own way and say: "I want *my* will to be done in this life. I want to live for me."

I believe this was the reason for Lewis that the doctrine of hell was so logical and just. He recognized that hell ultimately is the greatest of all monuments to human freedom. God gives all people what they want most, and that is to be free—even if they choose to be free from God Himself.

7

A LIFE OF CONTENTMENT

---❖---

If you are not happy with your life, you can change it in two ways: either improve the conditions in which you live, or improve your inner spiritual state. The first is not always possible, but the second is. —*Leo Tolstoy*

---❖---

Without exception, men have the capacity to scope out the future in their imaginations before it ever arrives. We are always questioning, *What if?* Envisioning the future can help us plan, can give us targets to shoot for, and can offer us realistic hope for a better tomorrow. Isn't it just as true that we are also at risk of spending too much of our time imagining a brighter future rather than living well in the present? As we play out the future in our imaginations, we often inadvertently throw our lives out of sync with present reality.

Isn't it just as true that we are also at risk
of spending too much of our time imagining a brighter
future rather than living well in the present?

As we have seen, the most obvious consequence in imagining the future is that it so easily leads to fear. Fear, worry, and anxiety all result from uncertainty. In the face of change and transition, we may start to worry about the unfolding of events yet to be realized, and this leads to a fear that can paralyze us as it starts to run wild in our imaginations. But most significantly, such fear can keep us from living a really good, joyful life in the present.

PLANNING TO BE HAPPY?

Another aspect of imagining the future proves to be troublesome for men, though generally we are totally unaware of it. Men seem to have this amazing tendency to arrange their lives around future expectations of happiness. Think about this for a moment. Doesn't this tendency of always contemplating a future life of happiness actually reveal something about our lives in the present—that we are unfulfilled and not content?

When we are not content, looking towards the future and hoping that it will be more satisfying than our lives today is only natural. We are convinced that one day we will be happy, yet our happiness always seems to remain just beyond the horizon.

Blaise Pascal clearly saw this tendency in people's lives:

We never keep to the present . . . we anticipate the future as if
we found it too slow in coming . . . We almost never think of the

present, and if we do think of it, it is only to see what light it throws on our plans for the future. The present is never our end.

Then he puts his finger on how most people live their lives:

Thus we never actually live, but hope to live, and since we are always planning how to be happy, it is inevitable that we should never be so.

One of C. S. Lewis' most popular books, *The Screwtape Letters,* is a novel in the form of a series of letters written by Uncle Screwtape to his nephew Wormwood. Screwtape and Wormwood are both demons. In these fictional letters, Screwtape gives advice to his nephew on how to contend with their enemy, who of course is God. The objective of Uncle Screwtape and Wormwood is to plot against and destroy the spiritual lives of people. They want to keep humans completely out of the enemy camp.

In one of the letters, Uncle Screwtape informs Wormwood that the enemy (God) wants people to learn how to live in and enjoy the present day. He tells his nephew that their goal is to prevent this. "It is far better to make them live in the Future," Screwtape tells Wormwood. As long as humans are living in their future imaginings, their lives are not in harmony with reality.

Uncle Screwtape then explains that God does not want people to give their hearts to the future and place their treasure and happiness in it, but he says, "We do." He concludes by saying that ultimately, "We want a whole race perpetually in pursuit of the rainbow's end, never honest, nor kind, nor happy *now* . . ."

Pascal and Lewis both recognized that one of the reasons we struggle to find meaning and joy in our lives is because no matter where we are in life, no matter how well things might be going for us right now, we always seem to be able to contemplate a better life in the future, better than what we are experiencing right now.

If you had the power to change certain circumstances right at this moment, wouldn't it be easy to imagine a life far more satisfying? As you think about your world right now, isn't there some way you can imagine improving it, making it better and more rewarding? Couldn't you be happier? Isn't there something that could make it better? As a very dispirited businessman shared with me recently, "I am desperately searching for a life of contentment."

When we are honest with ourselves, it is easy to see how we slip into the habit of always arranging and rearranging the future in our minds, always anticipating a better life in the not-too-distant future. Contentment is what we seek; and for most men, contentment will always be just around the next corner. Unfortunately, before we know it, life is over.

THE TYRANNY OF COMPARISON

What I have learned from so many men is that the real problem for us is that being content in the present is difficult. Very few of us are content with who we are, where we are, or what we have in this life.

Of course, one of the main reasons we are so discontent with our lives is because we are always comparing ourselves with others. We measure how well we are doing in comparison with others. We make mistakes and we feel inferior; we experience success and we feel superior. As we have seen, our emotions and our confidence moves with the market and flows with the opinion of others.

This is particularly true for men when economic hardship arrives. We all want to know how everyone else is doing. When we hear of other men who are faring much worse than we are, we feel a little better about ourselves. When we see others who seem to be totally unaffected by the recession, we experience a moment of deep despair. We are pulled by the twin poles of uncharitable thoughts, on the one hand, and envy on the other. And it can eat away at us.

R. C. Sproul says one sure indicator that reveals a person who is truly content with his life is when this person sees his friends and peers doing well and prospering and he rejoices with them. He is happy for them. On the other hand, when he sees them struggle and go through difficult times, he feels their pain and has great compassion for them. He hurts for them.

The noted Southern novelist and literary essayist Walker Percy is known for his peculiar talent in exploring the deeper questions of modern life relating to our habits, our self-deceptiveness, our fears, and our bewildering complexity. In one of his books, a spoof of modern life entitled *Lost in the Cosmos: The Last Self-Help Book*, Percy offers a humorous take on modern Western culture's obsession with pop psychology, which offers simple, untested answers to life's most difficult questions. In the book, Percy gives a battery of multiple choice tests as a reflection of the self-help quizzes that are so popular in many successful consumer self-help books and magazines. The questions are laced with moral challenges, often highlighted in humorous patterns, one of which I will paraphrase:

It is early morning and you are standing in front of your home, reading the headlines of the local newspaper. Your neighbor of five years, Charlie, comes out to get his paper. You look at him sympathetically—he doesn't take good care of himself and you know that he has been having severe chest pains and is facing coronary by-pass surgery. But he is not acting like a cardiac patient this morning!

Over he jogs in his sweat pants, all smiles. He has triple good news! "My chest pains," he crows, "turned out to be nothing more than a hiatal hernia, nothing serious." He has also just gotten word of this great promotion he has received and that he and his family will soon be moving to a new home, which happens to be in a much more exclusive part of town. Then, after a pause, he warbles on, "Now I can afford to buy the lake house we have always dreamed of owning."

Once this news settles in, you respond, "That is great, Charlie. I'm very happy for you."

Now, please fill in the following multiple choice. There is only one correct answer to each question.

Question: Are you truly happy for Charlie?

a. Yes, you are thrilled for Charlie; you could not be any happier for him and his family.

b. If the truth be known, you really don't feel so great about Charlie's news. It's good news for Charlie, certainly, but it's not good news for you.

Percy then gives the following directions:

If your answer to the question above is b, please specify the nature of your dissatisfaction. Do the following thought experiment—which of the following alternative scenarios concerning Charlie would make you feel better?

a. You go out to get your paper a few days later, and you hear from another neighbor that Charlie has undergone a quadruple coronary bypass and may not make it.

b. Charlie does not have heart trouble, but he did not get his promotion.

c. As the two of you are standing in front of your homes, Charlie has a heart attack, and you save his life by pounding his chest and giving him mouth-to-mouth resuscitation, turning his triple good news into quadruple good news. How happy would that make you?

d. Charlie is dead.

Percy then asks:

Just how much good news about Charlie can you tolerate?

Percy uses this exercise to flesh out the desires of our hearts. He wants to show us how we often compare ourselves to others.

109

But more significantly, Percy wants to show us how discontent we can be with our lives and that the reason for this discontentment is because we are always comparing ourselves with other people.

A LIFE OF CONTENTMENT

In perhaps the clearest and most direct passage in the Bible concerning man's striving for contentment, Matthew 6:25-34, Jesus says:

> *"For this reason I say to you, do not be worried about your life, as to what you will eat or what you will drink; nor for your body, as to what you will put on. Is not life more than food, and the body more than clothing?*
>
> *"Look at the birds of the air, that they do not sow, nor reap nor gather into barns, and yet your heavenly Father feeds them. Are you not worth much more than they?*
>
> *"And who of you by being worried can add a single hour to his life?*
>
> *"And why are you worried about clothing? Observe how the lilies of the field grow; they do not toil nor do they spin, yet I say to you that not even Solomon in all his glory clothed himself like one of these.*
>
> *"But if God so clothes the grass of the field, which is alive today and tomorrow is thrown into the furnace, will He not much more clothe you? You of little faith!*
>
> *"Do not worry then, saying, 'What will we eat?' or 'What will we drink?' or 'What will we wear for clothing?'*
>
> *"For the Gentiles eagerly seek all these things; for your heavenly Father knows that you need all these things.*
>
> *"But seek first His kingdom and His righteousness, and all these things will be added to you.*
>
> *"So do not worry about tomorrow; for tomorrow will care for itself. Each day has enough trouble of its own"* (author paraphrase).

A Life of Contentment

In the New Testament, as you read Paul's letters, you see a consistent theme on the importance of being content. Here's what Paul wrote in the book of Philippians:

> *I have learned to be content whatever the circumstances. I know what it is to be in need, and I know what it is to have plenty. I have learned the secret of being content in any and every situation, whether well fed or hungry, whether living in plenty or in want* (Philippians 4:11-12, author paraphrase).

Note that as Paul wrote this letter from prison, he did not know how long he would be there, nor did he know what the future held. I find it interesting that Paul says, in essence, "I have learned the secret of being content." When you tell someone you have learned a secret, what you are generally attempting to communicate is that what you have learned is not self-evident; it is not obvious and is not found where most people would look.

Paul makes it quite clear that his contentment was not based on outward circumstances. He says, "[I am] content in any and every situation, whether well fed or hungry, whether living in plenty or in want."

Back when the economy was booming, the stock market soaring, and the unemployment rate low, I would guess most of us felt rather content with life. But when the wheels started coming off and the economy cratered, I imagine the peace and good feelings we were experiencing deserted most of us.

So what had Paul learned that can help us in the here and now? What was his secret? As you read the book of Philippians, you will notice four distinct yet closely related perspectives that clearly contributed to Paul's life of contentment.

Contentment | Compared to what?

First, it strikes me that if the peace and contentment in our hearts are dependent on outside circumstances and how we compare with others, then we are in trouble because we have little or no control over so many of the situations we face. As we have seen, the truth is that comparing ourselves with others can never serve as a true measure of anything in an absolute sense, but only in a relative, temporal sense. Comparison as the sole measure of one's self-worth and happiness becomes the virtual death of contentment and peace.

Contentment | A man on a mission

Second, I believe Paul was able to draw upon all that he learned as a Pharisee before he had become a Christian. As a Pharisee having developed a great knowledge of the Old Testament, he would have been very familiar with Jeremiah 29:11, which speaks of the wonderful plan God has for each of our lives:

> *"For I know the plans I have for you," says the Lord, "plans for your welfare, not for calamity, to give you a future and a hope"* (author paraphrase).

Paul trusted God's plan for his well-being; he knew he had a future and a hope. Paul also knew that the reason most people never find that plan is because they are seeking to execute their own plans for their lives:

> *Woe to the obstinate children, declares the Lord, to those who carry out plans that are not mine . . .* (Isaiah 30:1, author paraphrase).

Therefore, Paul's contentment can be attributed to the fact that he lived his life with a sense of mission and calling. He understood and believed in God's good and sovereign hand on his life and circumstances. Paul understood that God had a purpose for him being in prison, and he was thus content to live in harmony with God's plan for his life.

For example, in Philippians 1:12-14, Paul speaks of how his imprisonment helped advance Christianity. He was overjoyed that so many more Christians "have been encouraged to speak the word of God more courageously and fearlessly." Nowhere in the book of Philippians do you see Paul complaining about his being locked up. Nor do you hear him say, "Once I get out of prison, then my life will be good." Paul was content sitting in prison in chains because he was convinced at that very moment, the good hand of God had him there for a reason, and his imprisonment was advancing God's kingdom.

If there is no meaning nor purpose behind difficult outside circumstances, then life will always be bleak and disappointing, especially when we go through trying times.

It is crucial to remember that if there is no meaning nor purpose behind difficult outside circumstances, then life will always be bleak and disappointing, especially when we go through trying times. Paul's example of commitment confirms that when we see meaning and purpose behind the struggles of life, our perspective will be transformed.

As we look at our lives today, is this the way we see ourselves?

Can we see purpose in our struggles, knowing that God, as promised, is using them in our lives? Are we right where God wants us spiritually? Are we seeking His plan for our lives?

Contentment | Life's great treasure

Third, I think Paul was content because he realized he had found life's great treasure. He speaks of this in a verse in Philippians, which we discussed in chapter five:

> *I consider everything worthless in comparison to the unsurpassing value of knowing Christ Jesus my Lord for who I suffered the loss of all things, and consider it rubbish, so that I might gain this relationship with Christ* (Philippians 3:8, author paraphrase).

If you'll recall, Paul had at one time been a wealthy, prominent Pharisee; but upon becoming a Christian, he had to give up everything. However, he reveals that all that he had to give up was rubbish when compared to the surpassing value of having a relationship with Christ.

I think most men actually believe material wealth is the source of contentment. Modern culture aggressively promotes this prevailing attitude. "When I have this much wealth" or "When I earn this level of income," then I will be content. Then, and only then, will life be good. I have had men sit across from me who have voiced their great contempt for God because they believe He has dealt them a bad financial hand. When they look at their friends and see how well they are doing, they are convinced that God has discriminated against them financially.

Yet God has indicated to us that material wealth is not all-important and, in fact, is not necessary for a person to be content. In 1 Timothy 6:7-8 Paul says:

*For we brought nothing into the world, and we can take nothing out
of it. But if we have food and clothing, with this we will be content*
(author paraphrase).

Paul is declaring that if we have our physical needs met, we can
find contentment. That is all that we basically need to be content.
Do we forget that the majority of us in the prosperous Western
world have far more than our basic needs being met? Therefore, we
are instructed to be grateful and to strive to be good stewards of
the resources we have been given.

In a letter to the church in Corinth (2 Corinthians 6:10), Paul
makes it clear that as far as material possessions went, he owned
nothing; yet in reality, he considered himself to be a wealthy man.
He was wealthy in the possessions that really matter in life. The
great treasure in Paul's life had been found in his relationship with
Christ. It was the one possession his heart had been looking for,
and therefore he was content.

Contentment | Death be not proud

Fourth, and finally, as I examine Paul's life, I am amazed at
how peaceful and content he was, even though he was always
facing grave danger. The specter of death hung over him every-
where he traveled because so many people wanted to see him dead.
It is truly remarkable to read in Philippians 1:21-23 where Paul
boldly declares that eternal life in the presence of God is in fact far
better than anything we can expect to experience in this earthly
life, which is full of pain and difficulty. In fact, Paul looked forward
to his death with great anticipation. He overcame the fear of death
through the tangible hope of eternal life, which in my opinion is
the primary reason he lived with such peace and contentment.

Though we go to great lengths not to think about it, the great obstacle to a life of peace and contentment is the natural fear of death. It is clearly our greatest enemy.

Dr. Armand Nicholi Jr., clinical professor of psychiatry at Harvard Medical School, has observed that the process of coming to terms with our mortality is extraordinarily painful. He contends that "the unbelievable brevity of our lives conflicts with our deep-seated yearning for permanence and with our lifelong fear of being separated from those we love—a fear that haunts us from infancy to old age."

I share Nicholi's assessment of the human condition. Our mortality is so distressing because of the realization that death separates us from those we love. We ultimately realize that we exit this life alone, and therefore, a sense of loneliness and fear grips us so powerfully.

Death is such a solitary experience.

And yet once again, here is another fear that men cannot share with others because admitting that we are fearful will only make us look weak. So we carry this burden around, increasing our sense of loneliness and alienation.

Have you ever wondered how different your life could possibly be if you were completely delivered from the fear of death? Take this a few steps further and ask, *What if I was delivered not only from the fear, but also was able to look forward to the day of my death with great anticipation? How would that change the life I am living right now?*

Of course most of us want to know if this was a true reality in Paul's life, and if so, how did he pull it off. I believe quite simply that Paul knew God intimately. He knew Him not just as God but also as his heavenly Father. Therefore, Paul saw death as more than simply going home; he saw it as going home to be with his Father. As he explains:

To be absent from the body is to be at home with the Lord
(2 Corinthians 5:8, author paraphrase).

This reminds me of a conversation I had with my oldest son just before he left for camp. This was the first time Dixon would be away from home for an extended period of time. I shared with him my own experience of going off to camp for the first time. I told him that it would go quickly, and that he would often think of home. I told him no matter how much fun he was having, he would deep down always be looking forward to the day he would come home. Finally, I told him the closer he got to the end, the more excited he would get because he would know that he would soon be going home; and home, of course, is where he belonged.

This is the way Paul lived his life. As he wrote from prison in Philippi, he knew that death was not far away. His excitement grew as he anticipated his homecoming. Of course, we should not be surprised that this is the way God desires for us to live as well.

WEARY AND HEAVY-LADEN

As I meet and talk with men and observe the struggles in their lives, I have come to realize that we all, deep down, are yearning for the same things. We all desire to be delivered from our fears. It can be quite tiring to live each day trying to impress others, always wondering, *What will people think of me?* And though we do everything we can to divert our thoughts from the fear of death, we are continually being reminded that we are mere mortals, and one day our lives will come to an end. We carry this invisible burden around silently, not really knowing what to do with it.

Jesus, with great compassion, knows and understands our burdens. He sees our pain. The Bible says that He sees us as sheep wandering through life without a shepherd. He says "Come to me, all who are weary and heavy-laden, and I will give you rest." Jesus knows us better than we know ourselves. He knows that deep down, each of us yearns for a life of contentment, where our hearts are at peace and our lives full of joy.

8

A TANGIBLE HOPE

It is a terrible thing to see but have no vision.

—*Helen Keller*

Helen Keller, a woman born deaf and blind, knew and understood that the only thing in life worse than being blind was not to have a vision for your life. "It is a terrible thing to see but have no vision," she said, and I could not agree with her more.

When a man, any man, catches a vision for what his life can really be, it transforms him. A vision for life truly changes a man and his response to the world around him; it changes him dramatically. As Stephen Covey says, "vision creates consequences."

THE LIFE THAT COULD HAVE BEEN

Many men, particularly in the face of difficult economic times, begin to seriously reflect and think about their lives. Though they may have been successful in their careers, they feel like they are drifting through life with no serious objectives.

Perhaps the greatest fear expressed in these moments of frustration is that, in the end, they are worried that they will have squandered their lives. They seem to be plagued in the back of their minds by the thought of the life that could have been.

I think we all reach certain junctures in our lives where we fear that we have not made much of a real difference. Consequently, we strongly feel the need to make some kind of change; but more often than not, these are nothing more than good intentions, which are of no real benefit in themselves.

As a prominent business leader lamented to Stephen Covey, "I haven't made a difference. I haven't taught my children to make a difference. I have basically been watching life go by through the hedges of my country club."

BEGIN WITH THE END IN MIND

Viktor Frankl, a noted Jewish psychiatrist, survived the Nazi death camps during World War II. Frankl was puzzled by the fact that some of his fellow prisoners wasted away and died, while others remained strong and survived. He looked at a number of different factors but finally concluded that the single most significant factor was their sense of a vision for their lives. Those who survived had a strong motivating conviction that they still had something significant to do with their lives. Frankl concluded that it was the power of this vision that kept them going.

I share this because, as I watch men out in the world of business, I have noticed how most of them live reactively rather than proactively. Their lives are little more than a series of reactions to the circumstances they are confronted with each day rather than a proactive life based on a vision of who they are and what they really want to accomplish. They clearly have no real plan or strategy to make life conform to their dreams and their goals. They yearn for a life of significance, yet most do not have the ability and sometimes even the motivation to see beyond their present reality. Few have developed a vision for their lives, and this explains why they just drift along each day.

Recently I had the opportunity to listen to an interview with Dr. Kevin Elko. Dr. Elko is a sports psychologist who works with professional and collegiate football teams, as well as many of the largest corporations in the world. (Here in the South he is quite popular having worked closely with the football teams at both LSU and the University of Alabama.) In this interview, he was asked about the message he delivers to his clients. He says his message is quite simple: people must choose to either live in their circumstances or be guided by a vision for their lives. He says that most people's lives are controlled by their circumstances, and therefore they allow other people's agendas as well as their own personal habits to control their lives. He too has experienced the reality that most men never establish a vision that will guide them into the future.

I first realized the significance of this almost nine years ago, as I was considering a career change. I was revisiting Stephen Covey's book, *The Seven Habits of Highly Effective People*, which I had read once before. As I began to look at the second habit—begin with the end in mind—it was as if a light bulb had finally turned on in my mind.

What this means is that as we consider our lives and our future plans, we must start with a clear understanding of our ultimate destination. Covey contends the best way to do this is to give serious thought to the legacy we leave behind. He asks us to consider a very effective thought experiment of attending our own funeral:

As you take a seat and wait for the services to begin, you look at the program in your hand. There are to be four speakers. The first is from your family, immediate and also extended—children, brothers, sisters, nephews, nieces, aunts, uncles, cousins, and grandparents who have come from all over the country to attend. The second speaker is one of your friends, someone who can give a sense of what you were as a person. The third speaker is from your work or profession. And the fourth is from your church or some community organization where you've been involved in service.

Now think deeply. What would you like each of these speakers to say about you and your life? What kind of husband, wife, father, or mother would you like their words to reflect? What kind of son or daughter or cousin? What kind of friend? What kind of working associate?

What character would you like them to have seen in you? What contributions, what achievements would you want them to remember? Look carefully at the people around you. What difference would you like to have made in their lives?

Covey believes this is the foundation that will enable us to develop a vision for our lives (or mission, as he likes to call it). Once we develop a well thought out vision, we then can begin to plot a course that will make sure it becomes a reality. Instead of wasting our lives and living reactively, we now have the criteria to measure everything we do in life, including our priorities, our choices, and the use of our time.

ISSUES OF THE SOUL

Unfortunately, most of us do not grow up thinking about a vision for our lives. We do not give much thought to the type of men we are becoming because we are so consumed with what we are achieving and what we are experiencing today.

We are seldom taught that the key
to experiencing a meaningful life is to make
a difference in the lives of others.

We are seldom taught that the key to experiencing a meaningful life is to make a difference in the lives of others. Far too rarely does a young man think seriously about the value of character, wisdom, or relationships. Peter Drucker observed that most men are underprepared for the second half of life and that there is no school or university to equip them for it.

Perhaps this explains why many men enter adulthood and just follow the herd (for what would others think of us if we chose to be different from everyone else). The poet E. E. Cummings expressed this quite well:

> We live in a world that is doing its best, night and day, to make [us] just like everybody else.

And this is, in fact, what happens to most men.

I guess you could say that most of us share the same vision; but unfortunately, it is the wrong vision, a vision based on how successful we can be in the visible, measurable dimensions of life. Over time we begin to realize that we cannot make sense of all the struggles we experience, private struggles concerning internal issues and spiritual questions that no one sees or talks about.

It is as if we live with a divided self. On the one hand, we have our outer public life, which everyone sees and judges us by. It is the part of our life that we feel compelled to manage well because it is the source, we believe, of our worth and identity. On the other hand, we have our private inner life, where what is truly going on within us remains hidden from the rest of the world.

This is not the life God intended for us. He is not interested or impressed with our public accomplishments and success. To the contrary, He is vitally interested about the type of men we are becoming. He cares most about the development of our hearts and the maturing of our souls.

God's will for us is that we be Christlike. This has nothing to do with being religious. In fact, the problem with religion is that it does not touch and impact our hearts. Too many men have somehow come to believe that Christianity merely involves our external behavior, such as going to church, attending Bible studies, or giving to charity. However, true Christianity focuses on the inner life; it is about the life of God working in the soul of man.

And this is so crucial to understand: all the struggles we have as men stem from issues of the soul. The soul is so important because it is the very life center of every human being. As Dallas Willard has noted, every man's soul is what is running his life at any given moment. Willard says that the soul is *deep* in the sense of being basic or foundational but also in the sense that it lies almost totally beyond conscious awareness.

Willard makes it very clear, however, that if we are going to be healthy and have our lives together, our souls must be properly ordered under God. He says that when our souls are in correct relationship to God, we as men will be "*prepared* for and *capable* of responding to the situations in life in ways that are good and right."

At its fundamental level, Christianity is relational—to know Jesus as a living reality. In knowing Him and deepening our relationship with Him, a process of transformation begins to take place. It is a transformation of our heart and soul at our core, our very center. In today's trying times, we are looking for anything that will make us feel better—anything that will fix us. God, however, desires to heal us, to restore us so that we might become the men He created us to be. And when this happens, it will impact every other area of our lives.

In today's trying times, we are looking for anything that will make us feel better—anything that will fix us. God, however, desires to heal us, to restore us so that we might become the men He created us to be.

THE REASON FOR LIFE

The early Greek philosophers lived during the same time period as a number of the Old Testament prophets. The Greek philosophers of the time developed a concept called the *logos*. It is where we get the English word *logic*. In Greek, the word logos literally means "the word"; but it has a secondary meaning, "the reason for life." The Greeks believed when one finds his logos, his reason for life, he would be complete and whole. He would then be able to reach his full potential as a person.

The problem is that the Greeks could never agree on what comprised the logos. They could never construct a unified belief on the reason for life. Rather than being "the word," logos became nothing more than "just another word."

This is why, Tim Keller says, that the apostle John, in his opening words in the gospel of John, drops a bombshell on the world:

In the beginning was the Logos,
And the Logos was with God,
And the Logos was God.
He was with God in the beginning.
All things came into being through Him
And apart from Him nothing came into being
That has come into being.
Life was in Him,
And that life was the light of men.
That light shines in the darkness,
Yet the darkness did not overcome it (John 1:1-5, author paraphrase).

God is revealing to us that in the beginning was the logos, the reason for life; and the reason for life was God, and the reason for life became a human being and dwelt among us. What John says is that the logos, the reason for life, was not and is not a philosophical principle, as the Greeks believed, but the logos is in fact a person, Jesus Christ.

When we enter into a relationship with Him and truly get to know Him and serve Him, we become complete and whole. We find a higher purpose for which to live. It is in Jesus Christ, indeed, that we discover our reason for life.

Afterword

IT ALL ADDS UP IN THE END

———————◆———————

Failure is simply an opportunity
to begin again, this time more intelligently.

—Henry Ford

———————◆———————

The Persona | REDUX

After twenty years of listening to the yearnings of people's
hearts, I am convinced that human beings have an inborn desire
for God. Whether we are consciously religious or not, this desire
is our deepest longing and most precious treasure. —Dr. Gerald
C. May

Remember the builder of *The Persona* in Gordon McDonald's
cautionary tale that began this book? Well, let's imagine that after
The Persona capsized in the storm, our foolish builder did indeed
survive. He was carried on a piece of flotsam by ocean currents
only to wash up on a deserted island lost in a remote expanse of

ocean far, far away from the civilized world. And yes, once he found himself on the island he realized just how fragile and lonely life can be without others.

Two Lost Souls, One Found

The author of Ecclesiastes reminds us that there is nothing new under the sun. Yet when we are willing to honestly search for the truth of life and in humility are willing to look to others for wisdom, we often find great examples and models to lead us in the right direction.

For my part, I would like to close this writing by turning to the generous knowledge and gifts of Beeson Divinity School professor Doug Webster, who wrote a very powerful essay that he shared with me. This essay serves to highlight the choices our foolish builder of *The Persona* is facing, now that we have imagined he is alive and struggling to survive on a deserted island.

Webster presents us with a brilliant example by way of counterpoint, comparing two well-known classics of lost souls on deserted islands—*Castaway*, the movie starring Tom Hanks, and *Robinson Crusoe*, the novel by Daniel Defoe. In the essay, reprinted below, Webster shows how each character's distinctive responses, although facing similar circumstances, present a radically different approach on how to deal with the struggles in life:

> In the movie *Castaway*, Tom Hanks plays Chuck Nolan, an efficiency expert for FedEx. His life consists of work and a relationship with a girlfriend. Just before he boards a FedEx flight to the South Pacific he proposes to her. He kisses her goodbye and assures her he'll be back in a week, but his plane goes down in a terrible storm and he washes up on a deserted island. He is the lone survivor and a modern day version of Robinson Crusoe. The differences between the movie *Castaway* and Daniel Defoe's

novel *Robinson Crusoe* illustrate the gap between survival and salvation, between a Christian life of faith and a modern [secular] view of life.

It is fitting that *Castaway* is a movie that looks at Chuck Nolan's struggle to survive, while *Robinson Crusoe* is a novel that explores the mind and soul of Crusoe. The medium itself says something about the modern person. That is not to say that novels don't depict a modern persona, but in the case of Robinson Crusoe, the novel captures his soul better than a movie could. In *Castaway*, we watch a familiar movie star act out a part. We comment to ourselves that Hanks looks heavy in the first half of the movie and about fifty pounds lighter in the second half of the movie. We make a mental note of his bleached hair and beard. From the odd assortment of FedEx packages that wash up on shore we question the value of our materialism. We watch him try to build a fire out of rubbing sticks and extract a tooth with the tip of an ice-skate. The only real clues as to what was on his mind [are] his habit of looking at his girlfriend's picture and his attempts to draw her likeness on the wall of a cave. When the body of the pilot washes up on shore, Nolan digs a shallow grave and buries the body. We see him standing before the mound, but instead of prayer, he comments, "That's that." The portrayal is entirely one-dimensional. It is a tale of survival. The greatest hint that Nolan is a relational being comes in the humor and pathos of his conversations with Wilson, conceived when Nolan's bloody hand print left a crude imprint of a face on a volley ball. The dialogue with Wilson is what the secular mind thinks of prayer: prayer is not real communion between God and the human person but a dialogue with one's own thoughts and feelings.

As the years drag on, Nolan contemplates suicide and becomes more like a caveman than a FedEx efficiency expert. He just barely clings to survival. Eventually, Nolan builds a raft and sails out to sea, to an almost certain death if it were not for the lucky break of being spotted by a tanker. He arrives home four years later to find his fiancée married. He has survived, but he cannot redeem the lost years and the lost relationships. The movie closes with Nolan standing at a four corner crossroads on the Texas panhandle as lost and directionless as he was on his deserted South Pacific island.

The contrast between *Castaway* and *Robinson Crusoe* could not be greater. In Defoe's novel, Crusoe emerges from his nearly three decades of isolation a much stronger person in the end than he was at the beginning. His experience on the isolated island proved invaluable. In the providence of God, his solitary life led him to examine himself. Suffering opened his heart and mind to God. Stripped of everything worldly, he saw himself as he really was, "without desire of good or conscience of evil." He began to lament his "stupidity of soul" and his ingratitude to God. Illness led him to pray for the first time in years, "Lord be my help, for I am in great distress." When he began to ask, "Why has God done this to me? What have I done to deserve this?" his conscience checked him. "Wretch! Ask what you have done! Look back upon a dreadful misspent life and ask what you have done. Ask, why you have not been destroyed long before this!"

Robinson Crusoe is much more than a story about survival. It is a story about salvation. Like the prodigal son, who ran off to the far country, squandered his inheritance, but came to his senses, Crusoe became deeply convinced and convicted of his wickedness. When he earnestly sought the Lord's help in repenting of his sins, he providentially came to the words in the Bible, "God exalted him to his own right hand as Prince and Savior that he might give repentance and forgiveness of sins to Israel" (Acts 5:31). He describes his reaction, "I threw down the book, and with all my heart as well as my hands lifted up to Heaven, in a kind of ecstasy of joy, I cried out aloud, 'Jesus, Thou Son of David, Jesus, Thou exalted Prince and Savior, give me repentance!'" Instead of praying for physical deliverance he prayed for the forgiveness of his sins. Deliverance from sin was "a much greater blessing than deliverance from affliction."

He [Robinson Crusoe] came to the sober conclusion that the transformation of his soul meant far more to him than his deliverance from captivity. "I began to conclude in my mind that it was possible for me to be more happy in this forsaken, solitary condition than it was probable I should ever have been in any other particular state in the world; and with this thought I was going to give thanks to God for bringing me to this place." Instead of a slow and fearful descent into despair, Crusoe experienced God's rhythms of grace. He read his Bible and prayed daily. He planted crops, made furniture, baked bread, built a canoe, and established an orderly, disciplined life. He lived a life of mercy, not sorrow, and his singular goal was to "make my sense of God's mercy to me."

The message of *Castaway* is that life is a solitary struggle for survival fueled by the human spirit and the existential self. Love, particularly romantic love, can be a great motivator, but relationships are often disappointing and not enduring. Loneliness and isolation expose the myths of modern life, and in the end we are directionless. The message of *Robinson Crusoe* is that life is a struggle in our soul between self-rule and God's will, and it can only come to resolution by the grace and mercy of God. Apart from the saving grace of the Lord Jesus Christ there is no hope, but with Christ we can experience an abundant life even in affliction and suffering.

THE TRUE MEASURE OF A MAN?

Many men approach the painful circumstances in their lives as events that they need to survive. Our attitude is generally, "Once I get through this, then my life will be good again, and then I will be happy." In the process we live out our days, allowing the unpredictable circumstance of life to dictate our sense of well-being. For most of us, it becomes a stressful, exhausting roller coaster ride. So we just keep going, never really getting it, disconnected from the truth of life.

However, this is never what God intended for us. Like Robinson Crusoe, God is trying to make a breakthrough in each of us through the painful struggles of life. As Tim Keller has observed, many men meet God only through a wilderness experience. We find ourselves in the wilderness (or being washed up on a deserted island), and we recognize that we are absolutely alone in a severely harsh environment.

It is through this wilderness experience that we finally wake up to the fact that what we have always looked to as our ultimate hope, the thing that has driven and motivated us, that one thing that makes us feel like real men, has deserted us. It has let us down; it can no longer be relied upon as our source of significance and security. However, being in the wilderness can be one of the great blessings of life because it is just in such a wilderness that we can finally discern what is true, what is real, what is authentic human existence.

As Robinson Crusoe eventually came to recognize with great clarity, his coming to know Jesus Christ personally meant far more to him than being delivered from the island. For in Christ he found a life of harmony and contentment—it was the life he had always been searching for, and he found it in the wilderness.

SELECTED SOURCES

Gratitude is not only the greatest of virtues,
but the parent of all the others.

—*Marcus Tullius Cicero*

Just as it takes a village to create a good citizen, it takes many diverse perspectives in many great books to create a social dialog that truly matters. The author would like to express his special thanks and gratitude to several people for granting permission to use their words to support and sustain this writing: Gordon MacDonald, Drayton Nabers Jr., and Doug Webster.

And, as with any writing and cultural learning, Christian or secular, the author humbly acknowledges that he too is simply standing on the shoulders of those who have come before. The author would also like to acknowledge his deepest appreciation of the many people whose writings have informed this work.

Anders, Max, General Editor; Moore, David George and Akin, Daniel L., Authors. *Holman Old Testament Commentary, Ecclesiastes, Song of Songs, Holman Reference.* Nashville: Broadman and Holman Publishers, 2003.

Blue, Ron and White, Jeremy. *Surviving Financial Meltdown: Confident Decisions in an Uncertain World.* Cambridge: Tyndale House, 2009.

Boorstin, Daniel J. *The Image: A Guide to Pseudo-Events in America.* Vintage Books Edition, 1992.

Brand, Dr. Paul, and Yancey, Philip. *Pain: The Gift Nobody Wants.* New York: Harper Collins Publishers, Zondervan, 1993, 68.

Buford, Bob, *Stuck in Half Time: Reinvesting Your One and Only Life,* Grand Rapids: Zondervan Publishing House, 2001, 132-133; and *Finishing Well: What People Who Really Live Do Differently!* Nashville: Integrity Publishers, 2004.

Collins, Jim. *Good to Great: Why Some Companies Make the Leap and Others Don't.* New York: HarperCollins Publishers, HarperBusiness, 2001, 21, 22, 28, 29.

Colson, Charles. *Kingdoms in Conflict.* Grand Rapids: Zondervan Publishing House, 1987, 68.

Covey, Stephen R. *The Seven Habits of Highly Effective People: Restoring the Character Ethic.* New York: Simon & Schuster, Inc., A Fireside Book, 1989; and with A. Roger Merrill and Rebecca R. Merrill. *First Things First: To Live, to Love, to Learn, to Leave a Legacy.* New York: Simon & Schuster, 1994, 50.

Crabb, Lawrence J. Jr. *Effective Biblical Counseling.* Grand Rapids: Zondervan Publishing House, Ministry Resources Library, 1977, 61; and with Don Hudson and Al Andrews, *The Silence of Adam: Becoming Men of Courage in a World of Chaos,* Zondervan Publishing House, 1995.

Flynt, Wayne. "Depression déjà vu for Birmingham." *Birmingham News* (March 22, 2009).

Foster, Richard J. *Celebration of Discipline: The Path to Spiritual Growth*, Revised Edition. New York: HarperCollins Publishers, HarperSanFrancisco, 1988.

Helliker, Kevin. "You Might as Well Face It: You're Addicted to Success." *The Wall Street Journal* (February 12, 2009), Health Journal.

Keller, Tim. Selected Sermons: "Man in the Wilderness," 1/8/06; "The Wellspring of Wisdom," 9/26/04; "Work and Rest," 3/23/03; "Sickness Unto Death," 9/14/03; and "The Search for Pleasure," 9/20/98.

Larson, Craig Brian. *750 Engaging Illustrations: For Preachers, Teachers, & Writers*. Grand Rapids: Baker Books, 2002, 478.

Lewis, C. S. *The Chronicles of Narnia, Book Six, The Silver Chair*. New York: Harper Trophy, HarperCollins Publishers, 1953; *Mere Christianity: An Anniversary Edition of the Three Books: The Case for Christianity, Christian Behaviour, and Beyond Personality*, edited and with an introduction by Walter Hooper. New York: Macmillan Publishing Co., Inc., 1952, 102; and *The Screwtape Letters With Screwtape Proposes a Toast*. New York: Macmillan Publishing Co., Inc., 1961, 68-71.

MacDonald, Gordon. *The Life God Blesses: Weathering the Storms of Life That Threaten the Soul*. Nashville: Thomas Nelson Publishers, 1994, xx-xxiii.

Manning, Brennan and Hancock, Jim. *Posers, Fakers, & Wannabes (Unmasking the Real You)*. Colorado Springs: Navpress, Think Books, 2003.

Marx, Jeffrey. *Season of Life: A Football Star, A Boy, A Journey to Manhood*. New York: Simon and Schuster, 2003, 70-73.

Miller, Arthur. *Death of a Salesman*. New York: Viking Press, Inc., Viking Compass Edition, 1949, 138.

Miller, Donald. *Searching for God Knows What*. Nashville: Thomas Nelson, Inc., 2004.

Moore, Peter C. *Disarming the Secular Gods: How to Talk So Skeptics Will Listen*. Downers Grove, IL: InterVarsity Press, 1989, 187-188.

Morris, Thomas V. *Making Sense of It All: Pascal and the Meaning of Life.* Grand Rapids, MI: William B. Eerdmans Publishing Company, 1992, 74.

Muggeridge, Malcolm, *A Third Testament.* Ballantine Books, 1976, 59.

Nabers, Drayton Jr. *The Case for Character: Looking at Character from a Biblical Perspective.* Tulsa, OK: Christian Publishing Services, 2006, 86-87.

Nicholi, Dr. Armand M. Jr. *The Question of God: C. S. Lewis and Sigmund Freud Debate God, Love, Sex, and the Meaning of Life.* New York: Free Press, 2002, 115-116.

Peck, M. Scott, M.D. *The Road Less Traveled: A New Psychology of Love, Traditional Values and Spiritual Growth.* New York: Simon and Schuster, A Touchstone book, 1978.

Postman, Neil. *Amusing Ourselves to Death: Public Discourse in the Age of Show Business.* New York: the Penguin Group, Penguin Books, 1986, vii-viii.

Rice, P. Brian. "Leadership Training," *Harvard Business Review,* The Leading Edge, LWCC, York, Pennsylvania.

Scelfo, Julie. "Men and Depression: Facing Darkness." *Newsweek* (February 26, 2007), 43.

Smith, Malcolm. Lecture Series, "The Search for Self Worth."

Solzhenitsyn, Alexander. *Gulag Archipelago II.* New York: Harper and Row, 1974, 613-615.

Thrall, Bill with Bruce McNicol and John Lynch. *TrueFaced, Trust God and Others with Who You Really Are.* Colorado Springs: NavPress, 2004, 33.

Thurman, Chris, Dr. *The Lies We Believe.* Nashville: Thomas Nelson, 1999, 32-33.

Wall Street Journal, February 12, 2009, "You Might as Well Face It: You're Addicted to Success," by Kevin Helliker, Health Journal.

Wells, David F., *Losing Our Virtue: Why the Church Must Recover Its Moral Vision*, William B. Eerdmans Publishing Company, 1998, 102.

Will, George. *The Washington Post* (July, 1990).

Willard, Dallas, *Renovation of the Heart: Putting on the Character of Christ*, NavPress, 2002, 199.

Yancey, Philip. *Where Is God When It Hurts?: A Comforting, Healing Guide for Coping with Hard Times*. Grand Rapids, Zondervan Publishing House, 1997, 142.

Zacharias, Ravi. *A Shattered Visage: The Real Face of Atheism*. Brentwood, TN: Wolgemuth & Hyatt, Publishers, Inc., 1990, 141.

STUDY GUIDE FOR *THE TRUE MEASURE OF A MAN*

The eight lesson study guide is ideal
for small group or individual study.
To download a complimentary study guide go to:
www.thecenterbham.org/our-books/

SPEAKING PROGRAMS WITH THE AUTHOR

Richard E. Simmons III welcomes inquiries
about speaking to various groups,
meetings and conferences.

FOR MORE INFORMATION

Contact Jimbo Head at
jimbo@thecenterbham.org